kiac

*Simple*

# GEOMETRIC QUILTING

# Simple
# GEOMETRIC QUILTING

## MODERN, MINIMALIST DESIGNS FOR THROWS, PILLOWS, WALL DECOR AND MORE

*Laura Preston,* FOUNDER OF VACILANDO QUILTING CO.

PAGE STREET
PUBLISHING CO.

PAGE STREET
PUBLISHING CO.

First published in 2019 by

Page Street Publishing Co.

27 Congress Street, Suite 105

Salem, MA 01970

www.pagestreetpublishing.com

Distributed by Macmillan, sales in Canada by The Canadian Manda Group.

23  22  21  20  19     1  2  3  4  5

ISBN-13: 978-1-62414-803-3

ISBN-10: 1-62414-803-4

Library of Congress Control Number: 2019931792

Cover and book design by Laura Gallant for Page Street Publishing Co.

Photography by John Ellis and Laura Preston

Cover image © John Ellis and Laura Preston

Printed and bound in China

# Dedication

For the brave and creative in all of us

Contents

# INTRODUCTION

I found quilting at the end of a long, frustrating search for a new artistic medium. I had been traveling around the United States in an Airstream trailer for a few months with my now husband and all my painting supplies, but never once picked up a brush. I studied painting and art history in college and was an oil painter for years, but the medium wasn't practical in a small mobile space. So, after exploring possibilities for a more useful creative expression, I came across a handful of modern quilters. I never knew quilts could look like works of art, and I was intrigued by this combination of craft, art, design and history. I had some rudimentary sewing skills, so I bought some fabric and improvised my first quilt. I had no idea what I was doing and poorly stitched everything by hand, but I was hooked. I learned everything I know about quilting from blog posts, tutorials and YouTube videos, and I haven't stopped making quilts since.

As a self-taught quilter who's spent hundreds of hours googling quilting techniques and learning from trial-and-error, I felt many resources lacked a truly comprehensive guide to take you step by step through the whole process of making a quilt—from design inspiration all the way to binding a quilt. With *Simple Geometric Quilting*, I want to teach you how to make each project in my unique style and create a holistic resource for all things quilting that you can reach for again and again, whether you're just learning how to quilt or have decades of experience making quilts.

Over the years I've developed my own style of quilting that focuses on simple, uncomplicated design and large geometric shapes. It's a style suited to beginners or those looking for a quicker quilting project—I've always tried to make my patterns with large-scale pieces of fabric and as little piecing as possible. This minimalist approach to quilting puts the focus on the shapes and departs from the traditional method of repeating identical blocks across the entire quilt. I still use traditional quilting techniques, such as hand quilting, and borrow from centuries-old designs—but I believe that to keep this craft alive, it has to evolve to stay relevant in the modern home.

All of my work is inspired by my travels and favorite places I've visited—the patterns in this book are no exception. I spent months looking through photos from my years of traveling, recalling some of the most memorable experiences, and distilling those experiences down into thoughtful, cohesive designs. At the end of each pattern, I share those stories with you to give you a sense of "why" behind the quilt and some insight into my design process.

With in-depth tutorials and twenty projects ranging from a small wall hanging to a large queen-size quilt, there's something for everyone who wants to learn how to make non-traditional quilts using traditional techniques. While these quilts, pillows and wall hangings may look simple, that doesn't necessarily mean they're easy. The four sections, squares and rectangles (page 26), triangles (page 54), curves (page 86) and combinations (page 120), start with the most straightforward piecing techniques and end with the most advanced. That said, I encourage you to give every project in the book a try, whether you're a sewing novice or a quilting expert.

I'd also like to encourage you to use the skills and techniques you learn in this book to create your own unique quilt designs. It can be intimidating when you're still learning, but if you're not quite sure where to start, read through the Design Notes sprinkled throughout the book to begin gathering inspiration, distilling a design, thinking about color and making it your own. The reason I wrote *Simple Geometric Quilting* was to inspire you and give you the confidence to make something that's truly you.

♡ Laura

# GETTING STARTED

Below is a list of essential tools that I use to make quilts. The specifics may vary from quilter to quilter and you may prefer using one brand over another, but you should be able to find all the supplies below at your local craft store or online.

## Tools

**Self-Healing Cutting Mat** – Bigger is better when it comes to the surface you cut your fabric on. I'd recommend nothing smaller than 18 x 24" (45.7 x 61 cm).

**Rotary Cutter** – You get the straightest, most accurate cuts by using a rotary cutter. I find 45 mm is best for all-purpose use and cutting multiple layers of quilting cotton.

**Acrylic Ruler** – These rulers come in all shapes and sizes, but as long as it's clear and straight, it'll work just fine to guide your rotary cutter when cutting your fabric. I get the most out of my 6 x 24" (15.2 x 61-cm) ruler.

**Straight Pins** – Also called ball head pins, these come in handy to keep fabric in place while piecing, especially when assembling half square triangles.

**Embroidery Scissors** – Small scissors with a pointy tip are perfect for snipping loose threads.

**Sewing Machine** – You don't need a fancy machine to make a quilt, especially when you're new to sewing. In fact, the machine I started my company, Vacilando, with was the most basic $90 Brother sewing machine with very few bells and whistles. As long as it has a straight stitch setting, it'll work for quilting!

**Sewing Machine Needles** – Refer to your sewing machine manual to find the proper size and type of needle you'll need for quilting, but make sure to have a few extra on hand in case your needle breaks.

**Thread** – My preferred thread for piecing and quilting is Coats & Clark Machine Quilt Cotton Thread, but any 100% cotton thread should do the trick when working with quilting fabrics.

**Iron and Ironing Board** – You'll need a reliable iron (no steam necessary) and a sturdy ironing board to press the seams of your quilt and iron the wrinkles out of your fabric.

**Starch Alternative** – To stabilize fabrics, help release wrinkles or give a slight stiffness while piecing or before basting, use a starch alternative when ironing. My favorite is Mary Ellen's Best Press.

**Fabric Marker** – Any type of disappearing ink fabric marker, tailor's chalk or painter's tape works just fine for marking your stitch lines on fabric, but the Clover Hera Marker is my favorite tool for marking on fabric. It makes sharp creases and never runs out!

**Curved Quilting Safety Pins or Spray Basting** – Depending on which method you use to baste your quilt, you'll need either curved safety pins or spray basting to temporarily attach the three layers of a quilt together before quilting. Regular safety pins will work, but the curved ones help catch all three layers of fabric.

**Painter's Tape** – Taping the edges of your backing fabric so that it's taut will help keep everything straight and smooth while basting.

## For Machine Quilting

**Walking Foot** – This attachment foot pulls both the top and bottom fabrics through the sewing machine at the same rate, which keeps your quilt layers from pulling or shifting while quilting. Your sewing machine manufacturer should make a walking foot that fits your machine.

## For Hand Quilting

**Thick Thread** – Depending on the look you want to achieve, you can use a wide variety of thread for hand quilting. I use Coats & Clark Cotton Crochet Thread size 10 which is quite thick and matte, but DMC Perle Cotton Thread is very popular and comes in many colors and thicknesses.

**Sashiko Needle** – These needles are longer, thicker and sharper than your standard needle. They are perfect for sewing multiple hand stitches with a thick thread. The eye is also bigger, which makes threading easier. I use long Clover sashiko needles.

**Leather Thimble** – There are many thimbles that can work for hand quilting, but I prefer a soft leather thimble that's more ergonomic and comfortable.

## Materials

With the right skills and a certain level of creativity, the possibilities are limitless when it comes to the materials you can use in a quilt. But there are some gold standards, especially when first starting out, for the best materials to work with when making a quilt.

I love working with all-natural fibers—mostly cotton and linen. Natural fibers are long-lasting, breathable, better for the environment and feel great against the skin. They're also extremely durable but get softer every time you use them. They may be a few dollars more per yard than the synthetic blends, but they'll last longer and feel better than the alternative.

After you get the materials for your quilt, you can choose whether or not to prewash your fabric. Prewashing your fabric will allow your fabric to shrink ahead of time and will result in a finished quilt with less crinkling and less shrinkage. If you decided not to prewash your fabric, your freshly finished quilt will look smoother and crisper until you wash it. After the first wash, it'll have that classic quilt crinkle. Personally, I don't prewash my fabric. Mostly because I'm impatient and want to make my quilts as soon as I get the fabric, but I also love how cozy snuggling under a crinkly quilt can be.

### Cotton

Quilting cotton is a high-quality 100% cotton that has always been my go-to fabric for making quilts. There are thousands of colors and prints to choose from, the fabric is tightly woven, shrinkage is minimal and the color doesn't typically bleed. It's also the easiest to work with, so I highly recommend beginners start with quilting cotton before moving onto any other materials. My absolute favorite quilting cotton is Robert Kaufman's Kona Cotton. There are 340 colors to choose from, it's relatively inexpensive and widely available. All of the quilting cotton used for the projects in this book is Kona Cotton!

### Linen

100% linen has a texture that's unmatched by any other material. It's nubby and rumpled, yet still looks sophisticated. It also breathes better than cotton, making it a great option for warm weather quilts. I love using it in quilts, but 100% linen is one of the trickiest fabrics to work with. Linen tends to shift around and is prone to fraying, so if you work with it, starch alternative and a wider seam allowance are necessary to keep your linen in check. But linen is all about embracing the wonky and imperfect.

Essex Linen, a 55% linen 45% cotton blend made by Robert Kaufman, is the best of both worlds—you get the look and feel of linen, but it's much easier to work with. There are a range of colors, textures, and even metallic options to choose from. I like working with their Yarn Dyed and Homespun collections—both are woven with two different color threads, but the weave of the Homespun is much more defined. Both of these types of Essex Linens are sprinkled into many of the projects in this book to add visual depth and texture when combined with the solid Kona Cotton fabrics. I encourage you to look for different varieties of linen and experiment with texture in your own quilts.

### Batting

Knowing which batting to get can be confusing with all the brands, fiber content combinations and words like "scrim" and "stabilizers." The most common batting type for quilting is cotton or a cotton/poly blend and both come in a variety of lofts (how thick the batting is).

Whichever batting you end up choosing, make sure to take note of the quilting distance recommended by the manufacturer. This is the farthest apart your quilting stitches can be to ensure your batting doesn't shift over time.

- 100% cotton is usually lightweight, drapes nicely, is breathable and perfect for year-round use. Because I prefer working with natural fibers, this is what I use in all of my quilts. I like Warm & Plush by The Warm Company. It's an extra thick 100% U.S.-grown cotton batting with no scrim (a stabilizer made of polyester).

- When you add poly into the mix, it usually gives your batting more loft, which makes for a fluffier quilt and accentuates your quilting design. 80/20 cotton/poly blend is a popular batting, which gives you the best of both worlds.

- Wool is another great option for batting if you want something extra-warm. It's typically more expensive, but it has a very high loft and is very warm and lightweight.

# BUILDING A QUILT

There's a standard order of operations when it comes to building a quilt. First, you cut and piece your quilt top, then iron and baste all three layers before stitching them together and finally bind the edges of your quilt. Follow these steps and helpful tips to learn the basic foundations of making any quilt.

## Piecing

The first step of making a quilt is piecing your quilt top together. Whether it's squares, triangles, curves or a combination of the three, you'll need to sew pieces of fabric together in order to create the design of the quilt. Traditional quilts are made up of blocks, or square units of patchwork shapes that are usually repeated to create the quilt top. A few of the projects in this book follow the traditional block method, but most of them, like many modern quilts, use a non-traditional, freeform construction method.

Squares and rectangles (page 26) are the most simple, straightforward shapes, and they are a great place for beginners to start. The piecing of triangles (page 54) and curves (page 86) is more complex, so I've provided Technique Tutorials to help you master those shapes. In the last chapter, I cover combination quilts (page 120), so feel free to reference all the techniques in the book as you create these geometric quilts with a full toolbox of shapes.

### Piecing Tips

- I refer to the right side and the wrong side of the fabric in many of the patterns. The right side is the top, front-facing side. The wrong side is the back side of the fabric. For all piecing, you want your stitches to be on the wrong side of the fabric so your thread and seam allowance are hidden on the back side. That means when you're piecing, the right sides of the fabric will be facing each other.

- The seam allowance for piecing is always ¼" (6 mm). Many sewing machines come with a ¼" (6-mm) foot where you can use the edge of the foot as a guide for the edge of your fabric. Measure the distance from your needle to the edge of your foot to make sure it's ¼" (6 mm).

- Use a shorter stitch for piecing to make sure your seams are tight and sturdy. I usually set my stitch length to 2.0 (2 mm).

- Gently guide your fabric through your machine, letting the machine do all the work. Don't pull or push it through, otherwise you can warp your fabric and mess up your stitch length.

- Press your seams after piecing the blocks or strips of your quilt, either with your finger or the tip of your iron. There are two ways to press your seams: open or to the side. Both have their benefits and people have strong preferences in both directions. My suggestion is to try both and see which one you like best!

  - OPEN: To press your seams open, use either an iron or your finger to open the seam and lightly press it open. I prefer to press my seams open, as I'd rather them all be the same instead of worrying about which direction to press my seams.

  - TO THE SIDE: To press your seams to the side, use an iron to gently press your seam to one side—usually toward the darker fabric. Keep in mind that you'll need to alternate the direction of the seams that meet at an intersection and "nest" them in order to reduce bulk.

- If you're working with 100% linen, use a wider seam allowance. Because linen is a looser weave and more prone to fraying, it's best to use a ½" (12-mm) seam allowance to avoid your linen coming apart at the seams.

# Ironing + Basting

When you've completed your quilt top, you'll need to iron it along with the backing fabric to smooth out any wrinkles and make sure all your seams are pressed and flat. The next step is basting your quilt, where you temporarily attach the three layers (top, batting and backing) together with pins or spray adhesive to hold it together while you're quilting.

1. To make sure your quilt lies flat and smooth, it's important to press your seams and iron your quilt top and backing. I set my iron to the highest setting for ironing cotton and linen, but you should check what your iron recommends for the fabric you're using. I like to use a starch alternative (see the Tools section on page 11) with a dry iron—the starch will help to release the wrinkle and give your fabric a bit more stiffness, which makes it easier to baste your quilt. Iron your quilt top on the wrong side, making sure all your seams are pressed and intersections are as flat as possible. Let the weight of the iron do all the work. When you've ironed the top smooth on the wrong side, turn it over to the right side and give it a final press. Do the same with your backing fabric.

2. Next, you'll make a "quilt sandwich" by stacking and temporarily attaching your three layers—backing, batting and quilt top—together so you can quilt your quilt. There are two common ways to baste a quilt: using safety pins or a spray fabric adhesive. They each have their benefits and drawbacks (see below). Try either or both and see which works best for you!

I personally prefer pin basting, so these steps are based on that method.

3. Find a table or floor space large enough to lay out your entire quilt. Start by spreading out your backing fabric, wrong side facing up, and working from the middle outwards, smooth out all the wrinkles and bubbles. When your backing fabric is as smooth as possible, tape along all four edges with painter's or masking tape, pulling the fabric slightly taut as you go.

4. Then, lay your batting out on top of your backing fabric, making sure to line up the edges as best as you can. Smooth your batting from the middle outwards taking care not to shift your backing fabric underneath.

5. Finally, spread your quilt top out on top of the batting, leaving a few inches of batting sticking out around each edge. Carefully smooth your quilt top from the middle outwards until all wrinkles, creases and bubbles are gone and the quilt top lies as flat as possible.

6. Take your safety pins and pin all three layers together every 4 inches (10 cm) or so. When you've pinned your entire quilt top, carefully remove the tape from around the backing fabric, and roll or fold your quilt sandwich up to move it back to your sewing machine.

| Method | Pros | Cons |
|---|---|---|
| Safety Pins | • Reusable<br>• Better for your health and the environment<br>• Inexpensive | • Time-consuming<br>• Sharp points can prick you<br>• Fabric can shift while quilting |
| Spray Baste | • Much faster<br>• Firmer hold<br>• No pin holes | • Expensive<br>• Contains chemicals<br>• Can be messy/sticky |

# QUILTING 101

## Design

Your quilting design is the pattern you create with your quilting stitches. This design can complement your quilt top by following its lines and shapes or it can be a different design altogether to create another dimension to your quilt. Your quilting design can include a lot of quilting, which will give it a lot of texture, or you can quilt minimally and let the quilt top design shine. Whichever style you decide, make sure to check the maximum quilting distance on your batting—most range from 3 to 10" (7.6 to 25.4 cm). This is the maximum distance apart your rows of quilting can be.

If you decide to hand quilt, your quilt design options are limited only by how much time you want to spend hand quilting. You aren't bound by the limitations of a machine, and you can design your quilting pattern any way you like. Keep in mind that the more complex and close together your hand quilting pattern is, the longer it will take to finish.

If you're a beginner and decide to machine quilt on your domestic sewing machine, I'd recommend keeping the design simple to avoid having to man-handle your quilt through the machine. Anything with angles requires adjusting the position of the quilt relative to your machine without lifting your needle and then rerolling; this can be awkward and time-consuming. Straight rows or a crosshatch design are typically a good place to start.

To transfer your quilting design to your quilt top, use your ruler and Clover Hera Marker to mark creases where you want your stitches to be. This ensures that your rows are straight and even. If you don't have a Hera Marker, you can use the dull edge of a butter knife, tailor's chalk or even painter's tape. You'll use the creases as a guide for your quilting rows.

## Choose a Quilting Method

There are two main ways of quilting a quilt: by hand or by machine. Both have their pros and their cons, and the method you choose depends on your skills and aesthetic preference.

| Method | Pros | Cons |
| --- | --- | --- |
| Hand Quilting | • Beautiful, heirloom finish<br>• More forgiving and easier to begin with if you aren't comfortable with your machine yet | • More time-consuming<br>• More delicate—hand washing or dry cleaning is recommended |
| Machine Quilting | • Much faster<br>• More durable and can handle machine washing—best with kids and pets | • Fabric can shift and pucker more easily<br>• Larger quilts can be difficult to sew on a domestic machine |

When I first taught myself to quilt, I wasn't very confident on my sewing machine and didn't have a walking foot, so I started out with hand quilting. It took some practice to get comfortable with the technique and the rhythm, but the method was much more forgiving functionally and aesthetically. I hand quilted exclusively for two years until I finally gave machine quilting a try. Machine quilting is definitely much faster and more durable, but I still love the meditative process of hand quilting.

Whichever method you choose, I'd recommend making some test swatches before you start on your first project. Make a mini quilt sandwich with some scraps, and try machine quilting a few rows of stitches or sew a few hand-quilted shapes to get the feel for it.

If you're going with hand quilting continue reading. If you're machine quilting, skip to page 21.

## Hand Quilting

If you've decided to hand quilt, you'll need the thimble, needle, thread and small scissors listed in the Tools section on page 11. Many hand quilters use a hoop to keep their quilt sandwich taut, but it's not necessary.

To start, cut a length of thread within your arm span. Thread your needle and tie a quilter's knot (or a triple knot if a quilter's knot sounds intimidating) at the other end. Place your thimble on the middle finger of your dominant hand.

From the underside of your quilt, stick your threaded needle through the back of the quilt, bringing the needle up through the quilt top in the spot where you want to start your first row. Pull the thread through and tug slightly to pop your knot through the backing fabric, but not all the way through the batting. This hides the knot inside the quilt.

While you're quilting, use your non-dominant hand underneath the quilt to support the fabric while you're stitching. Be careful not to prick yourself with the needle.

*Mark the quilting rows with your Hera marker.*

Hold the needle between your thumb and forefinger and stick your needle back down through the top of the quilt, but not all the way through. Then, place your thimbled finger at the end of the needle, and use a rocking motion to push the end down and the tip back up through the quilt sandwich from the bottom. Use your thumb to push against the fabric and slide the needle through. This creates your first stitch!

Using the method above, you'll continue stitching to create a "running stitch" that follows the lines of your quilting design. Instead of doing one stitch at a time, "load" up your needle with two to four stitches and then pull the thread all the way through.

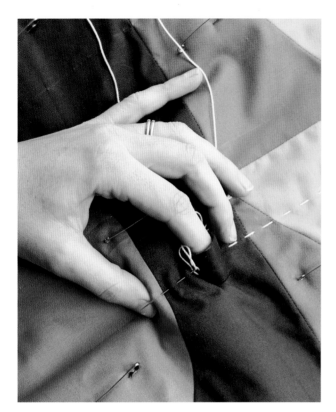

*"Loading up" your needle with multiple stitches speeds up hand quilting.*

Tip: When you first start, your stitches will probably be large, uneven and wonky—that's totally okay! That only adds to the character of the quilt. The more you practice, the smaller, straighter and more even your stitches will become. Although, even after years of hand quilting, my stitches still have a healthy amount of wonkiness to them.

NOTE: There are a few types of hand quilting: traditional hand quilting, big stitch and sashiko.

- When I think of traditional hand quilting, I think of Amish quilts. These stitches look almost like machine quilting, they're so small and even. This method typically uses a thin thread and extremely small stitches, anywhere from 8 to 12 stitches per inch (2.5 cm) by some of the most advanced quilters.

- Big stitch quilting is bolder and uses a thicker embroidery thread with 2 to 4 stitches per inch (2.5 cm). It's more freeform and forgiving with fewer guidelines. This is the method I started out with.

- Sashiko is a traditional Japanese technique of hand sewing that uses decorative stitches for mending and quilting. The stitches are made in a 3:2 proportion, with the longer stitch on the top of the quilt. The patterns and rules of sashiko are very specific, but the overall effect is striking.

## Machine Quilting

If you've decided to machine quilt your quilt, you'll need to swap out the regular sewing foot with a walking foot as instructed by your sewing machine manual.

Before you start, lay your quilt sandwich flat and then roll both edges of your quilt sandwich in toward the middle, making sure your rolls run parallel to your quilting lines. Rolling your edges ensures that your quilt will fit neatly through the throat of your sewing machine. This isn't always necessary, especially if your quilt is small or you're doing a more complex quilting pattern, but it will make the machine-quilting process a whole lot easier.

Continue quilting until you have about 6" (15.2 cm) of thread remaining. With your thread coming up through the quilt top, carefully tie a triple knot close to the quilt top, approximately one stitch length from where it comes out of the fabric. Then, make your last stitch by sticking your needle down and then back up through just the quilt top and the batting, but not through the backing. Tug slightly on the end of the thread to pop your knot underneath the quilt top and batting to secure it in place. Snip the end of your thread and make sure the end is buried underneath the quilt top. Repeat until your entire quilt is quilted.

*If your machine has adjustable presser foot pressure, you can always machine quilt with a normal foot on the lowest pressure setting.*

Adjust the stitch length on your machine to longer than what you'd use for piecing, between 3 and 4 millimeters or 6 to 8 stitches per inch (2.5 cm).

The easiest method I've found to machine quilt is to start from the middle and work your way out. This moves any shift of fabric toward the outer edges, as opposed to locking any bubbles or creases in the middle of the quilt. Starting with the center quilting row, stitch right down the center of the crease from one edge to the other, backstitching at each end to secure. When you get to the end of that row, snip your thread and go back to the top, starting with the next row to the right.

Continue stitching each row to the right of the last one, unrolling the right roll and rolling the left roll inwards, until you reach the right edge of the quilt. At this point, you should have one half of your quilt sandwich quilted.

To quilt the other side, lay your quilt flat again and reroll your edges as you did in the beginning. Then you'll repeat the same steps as above on the unquilted side, quilting each row from the center to the right. This means you'll be starting your rows from the bottom and ending at the top.

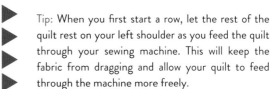

Tip: When you first start a row, let the rest of the quilt rest on your left shoulder as you feed the quilt through your sewing machine. This will keep the fabric from dragging and allow your quilt to feed through the machine more freely.

# Binding

### Step 1: Trim + Square the Quilt

When you've finished quilting, it's time to bind your quilt! This step hides the raw edges and creates a nice finished look. Binding is a multi-step process that begins by trimming the edges of your quilted quilt. You'll want to use your ruler and rotary cutter to cut the excess batting and backing off. Ideally, the dimensions will be the same as the finished dimensions, but if you need to trim down a bit more to make your edges straight and corners square, that's just fine.

### Step 2: Sew the Binding Strips Together

To make your binding, you'll start by cutting multiple 2½" (6.3-cm) x WOF (width of fabric) strips from your binding fabric and trim the selvedge off. Then take the short ends of two strips with right sides together and position the top strip perpendicular to the one below, lining up the corners. Sew diagonally from the top left corner to the bottom right corner. Trim the excess fabric, leaving a ¼" (6-mm) seam allowance and press the seam open. Repeat the steps above with the remaining strips until they're all connected.

Once all the strips are joined, fold the strip in half lengthwise with the wrong sides facing and press with your iron. Unfold one end of your binding strip and using your ruler and rotary cutter, cut the top left corner off at a 45-degree angle. Fold that end back in half.

### Step 3: Attach the Binding to the Quilt Front

Take the cut end of your binding strip and place it on the front side of your quilt with the raw edges of the strip aligned with the edge of your quilt, about half way down one of the sides. Leave a 6 to 8" (15.2 to 20.3-cm) tail and slowly stitch the binding strip to the front of the quilt with a ¼" (6-mm) seam allowance.

When you reach a corner, stop ¼" (6 mm) away from the edge and backstitch a couple times to strengthen the corner. Without breaking your thread, lift the presser foot and rotate your quilt to start along the new edge. Raise your needle and fold the binding up and away from the quilt so it's perpendicular to the previous edge. Maintaining that first fold, fold the binding back down on itself so the binding edge lines up with the new edge of the quilt. Place your presser foot back down and continue sewing down the new edge with a ¼" (6-mm) seam allowance, backstitching a few times at the corner to secure. Repeat until you've sewn along all edges and around corners.

*Step 1*

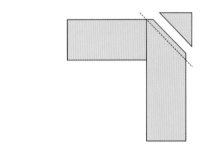

*Step 2.1*

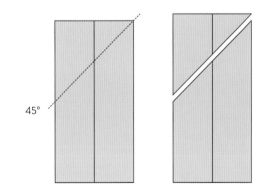

45°

*Step 2.2*

When you get close to where you started, stop stitching about 6 to 8" (15.2 to 20.3 cm) from the end of the beginning tail. Unfold the beginning and end tails of your binding strips, layering the beginning tail on top of the end tail, making sure there's no slack between the two. Pin the unfolded tails to the edge of the quilt. Using the 45-degree angle you cut out of the beginning tail, mark the line where the two ends overlap on the end tail with your ruler and Hera Marker. Unpin and using the line you just marked, cut a 45-degree angle with a ½" (12-mm) allowance.

Then, with the right sides of your beginning and end tail, sew the two ends together with a ¼" (6-mm) seam allowance. Press the seam open, refold the binding and finish sewing around the rest of your quilt until all the binding is attached to the front.

## Step 4: Attach the Binding to the Quilt Back

Flip your quilt over so the backside is facing up and turn your binding so the folded edge wraps around the raw edge of the quilt. Some people like to clip or pin their binding in place while they attach it to the backside. I use one or two craft clips and move them down as I sew.

There are two ways to sew your binding to the backside of your quilt: by hand or by machine. By hand is much slower and not quite as durable, but it's more forgiving. Machine is quicker, but the potential for slipped, wiggly stitches is much higher. If you're just starting out I'd recommend sewing by hand and will instruct based on that method.

Using the same thread (approximately a 24" [61-cm] length is most manageable), a small universal needle and a leather thimble, make a quilter's knot or a quadruple knot at the end of your thread. Tuck that knot into the quilt back close to the edge so the binding hides it, making sure it's securely fixed. Then, push your needle up through the very edge of your fold, pull the thread through and bring the needle down through the backing and batting only, right below where your binding stitch is. Push the needle back up through the backing and batting, about ½" (12 mm) away from the first stitch, and then catch the very edge of your fold right above where your needle came out. Continue these stitches, pulling your thread taut as you go. When you get to a corner, you'll fold the binding into a mitered corner and do a triple stitch to secure.

When you near the end of the thread length, make a knot, stitch through the backing and batting and pop the knot through both layers. Trim the tail off. Repeat until your entire quilt is bound.

*Step 3.1*

*Step 3.2*

*Step 4*

Starting Out
with Squares +
Rectangles

SQUARES AND RECTANGLES are the foundations of many quilt blocks and the perfect introduction to quilting. Because the construction is simple and straightforward, it's the best way for a beginner to get comfortable with the sewing machine and the basics of piecing a quilt top together. When I started teaching myself how to quilt, I decided to use only squares and rectangles for my first two quilts for that very reason—it was the easiest place to start and gain confidence in my sewing skills.

Using squares and rectangles in a design can create some of the most striking minimal quilts. While the shape is classic and bold, you can dictate the vibe of the quilt with the colors you choose—high-contrast colors make for a bold, assertive quilt, while warm tonal colors like the Antelope Canyon Throw (page 43) are soft and relaxing. Whether it's repeating the same shapes across the Hill Country Queen Quilt (page 49), using rectangles to create movement in the Abiquiu Crib Quilt (page 39), or combining different sizes and variations with the Kalaloch Pillow (page 29), the possibilities of how to use squares and rectangles in a quilt are limitless.

In this section, you'll learn the basics of piecing squares and rectangles into a quilt top, and how to apply those skills to the following five patterns that range from a wall hanging to a queen-size quilt. You'll also learn ways to tweak the designs and colors to make it your own, as well as helpful tips and tricks to piece more quickly and accurately.

**INSPIRED BY PILES OF DRIFTWOOD** on the Washington coastline, I love the Kalaloch Pillow because the design looks complex, but the construction is fairly simple. Sewing together larger blocks, cutting them down into smaller strips and then piecing them back together, creates an impressive and visually interesting design. I find that quilted pillows can look flat and bland, but with the small, seemingly random rectangles in a mix of cotton and textured linen, this one is anything but boring.

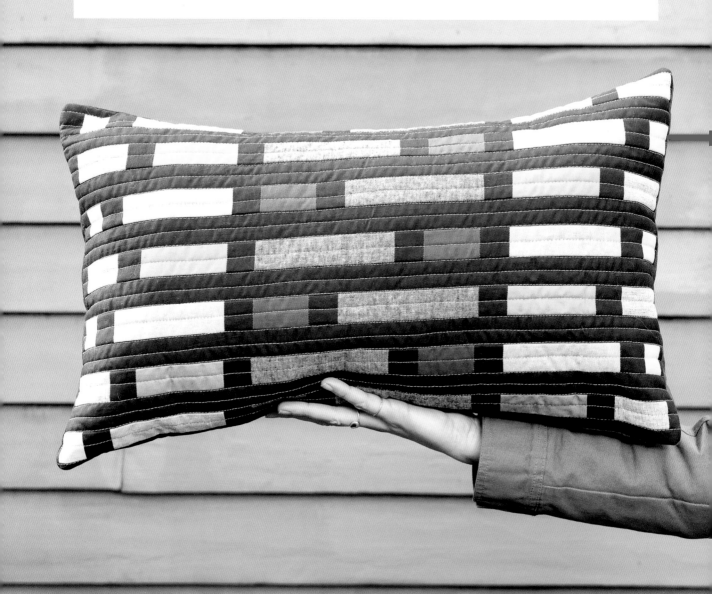

# KALALOCH PILLOW

14 x 24" (35.5 x 61 cm)

| Fabric | Yardage | # of Pieces | Dimensions |
|---|---|---|---|
| Navy | 1 yard (0.9 m) | 8 | 1½ x 25" (3.8 x 63.5 cm) |
| | | 7 | 1½ x 10½" (3.8 x 26.7 cm) |
| | | 2 | 14½ x 16" (36.8 x 40.6 cm) |
| Indigo Linen (Yarn Dyed) | ¼ yard (0.2 m) | 1 | 5½ x 11" (14 x 27.9 cm) |
| Steel Linen (Yarn Dyed) | ¼ yard (0.2 m) | 1 | 4½ x 11" (11.4 x 27.9cm) |
| Charcoal Linen (Homespun) | ⅛ yard (0.1 m) | 1 | 2½ x 11" (6.3 x 27.9 cm) |
| Medium Blue | ⅛ yard (0.1 m) | 1 | 3½ x 11" (8.9 x 27.9 cm) |
| Dark Blue | ⅛ yard (0.1 m) | 1 | 2½ x 11" (6.3 x 27.9 cm) |
| Fog | ⅛ yard (0.1 m) | 1 | 1½ x 11" (3.8 x 27.9 cm) |
| Batting | 16 x 26" (40.6 x 66 cm) | | |
| Pillow Insert | 16 x 26" (40.6 x 66 cm) | | |

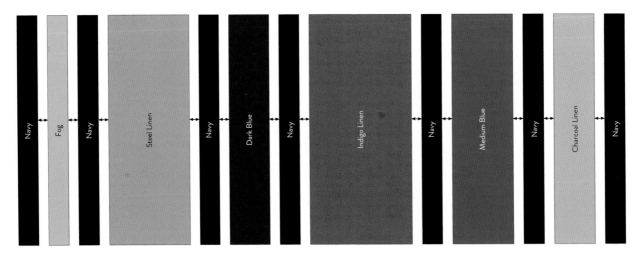

*Step 2.1*

## Step 1: Cut the Fabric

1.  Using your rotary cutter, ruler and cutting mat, cut all your fabric according to the chart on page 29. For your Navy fabric, I recommend cutting your yardage to 25" (63.5 cm) x WOF and then cutting the strips width-wise. Set the two 14½ x 16" (36.8 x 40.6-cm) Navy rectangles aside for assembling the pillow back later.

## Step 2: Assemble the Strips

Start by laying out your strips on your workspace the order shown above.

1.  Sew the strips together along the long edge with a ¼" (6-mm) seam allowance. When all thirteen strips are sewn together, flip the block over and press all your seams open with the tip of your iron.

2.  After you've pressed your seams open, use your ruler and rotary cutter to cut seven 1½" (3.8-cm) strips from the length of your block. Lay out all seven strips on your workspace, flipping every other strip around to face the opposite direction.

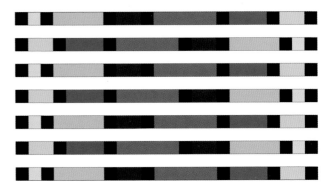

*Step 2.2*

## Step 3: Complete the Pillow Top

1.  With all seven of your pieced strips laid out and facing the right directions, you'll sew a 1½ x 25" (3.8 x 63.5-cm) Navy strip between each one along the long edge, starting at the top with a Navy strip and adding the next row down as you go. Take care to not stretch the pieced strips as you sew them to the Navy strips. You should start and end with a Navy strip.

2.  When you've sewn all fifteen of the strips together, carefully press all your seams open.

## Step 4: Finish the Pillow

1. Make sure all seams are pressed open, and iron to smooth the pillow top and backing fabric. The backing fabric will be on the inside of the pillow, so feel free to use any 16 x 26" (40.6 x 66-cm) piece of fabric you have. Following the steps on page 16, baste and quilt using your favorite method, then trim your top down to 14½ x 24½" (36.8 x 62.2 cm).

2. Take the two 14½ x 16" (36.8 x 40.6-cm) Navy rectangles and hem each piece along the short edge. To do that, fold the short edge over ½" (12 mm) and press flat. Then fold another ½" (12 mm) and press. Sew along the edge of your first fold, securing the hem. Repeat with the second piece of backing fabric.

3. Next, place your pillow on your workspace with the right side facing up. Take one of your hemmed pillow back pieces and place it on top with the right side (the smooth side of the hem) facing down. Line up the raw short edge with the right side of your pillow top. Do the same with your other backing piece, but align the raw short edge with the left side of the pillow top. Your two backing pieces should overlap by a few inches. Pin around the edges, and sew with a ¼" (6-mm) seam allowance all the way around the rectangle. Then trim the corners at an angle to reduce bulk, and turn your pillow right side out. Stuff with a 16 x 26" (40.6 x 66-cm) pillow insert, and you're done!

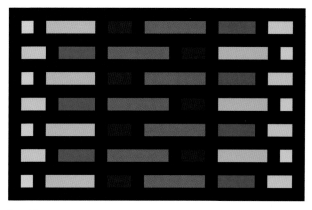

*Step 3.2*

## Inspiration

Along the remote coast of the Olympic Peninsula, there's a beach called Kalaloch. It's sandy and long, flanked by short cliffs and is riddled with driftwood. Not small driftwood—giant trees that have fallen into the ocean and then washed up onto the beach to age and weather. Hundreds of them are piled up, every one unique in color and shape, and all together they create an impressive forest of a different sort. By using different colored fabrics in different lengths and arranging them in a random, yet ordered, pattern, they mimic the giant driftwood trees on the Washington coast.

**THE ATASCADERO WALL HANGING** takes the traditional log cabin quilt block and restructures it into an unexpected pennant shape that's perfect as a wall hanging. I pictured the Atascadero Wall Hanging in a light-filled home that exudes "California cool," which led me to the sunny, golden hour colors, classic but modern shape and minimalist matchstick quilting.

# ATASCADERO WALL HANGING

19 x 29" (48.3 x 73.7 cm)

| Fabric | Yardage | # of Pieces | Dimensions | Name |
|--------|---------|-------------|------------|------|
| Tan | ¼ yard (0.2 m) | 2 | 2 x 2" (5 x 5 cm) | T1 |
| | | 3 | 2 x 3½" (5 x 8.9 cm) | T2 |
| | | 3 | 2 x 5" (5 x 12.7 cm) | T3 |
| | | 2 | 2 x 6½" (5 x 16.5 cm) | T4 |
| | | 2 | 2 x 8" (5 x 20.3 cm) | T5 |
| | | 3 | 2 x 9½" (5 x 24.1 cm) | T6 |
| | | 3 | 2 x 11" (5 x 27.9 cm) | T7 |
| | | 2 | 2 x 12½" (5 x 31.7 cm) | T8 |
| | | 1 | 2 x 14" (5 x 35.6 cm) | T9 |
| Curry | ⅛ yard (0.1 m) | 3 | 2 x 2" (5 x 5 cm) | C1 |
| | | 2 | 2 x 3½" (5 x 8.9 cm) | C2 |
| | | 1 | 2 x 5" (5 x 12.7 cm) | C3 |
| Yarrow | ⅛ yard (0.1 m) | 1 | 2 x 5" (5 x 12.7 cm) | Y1 |
| | | 3 | 2 x 6½" (5 x 16.5 cm) | Y2 |
| | | 3 | 2 x 8" (5 x 20.3 cm) | Y3 |
| | | 2 | 2 x 9½" (5 x 24.1 cm) | Y4 |
| | | 1 | 2 x 11" (5 x 27.9 cm) | Y5 |
| Gold | 1 yard (0.9 m) | 1 | 2 x 11" (5 x 27.9 cm) | G1 |
| | | 3 | 2 x 12½" (5 x 31.7 cm) | G2 |
| | | 2 | 2 x 14" (5 x 35.6 cm) | G3 |
| | | 3 | 2½" (6.3 cm) x WOF | Binding |
| | | 1 | 21 x 31" (53.3 x 78.7 cm) | Backing |
| Batting | 21 x 31" (53.3 x 78.7 cm) | | | |

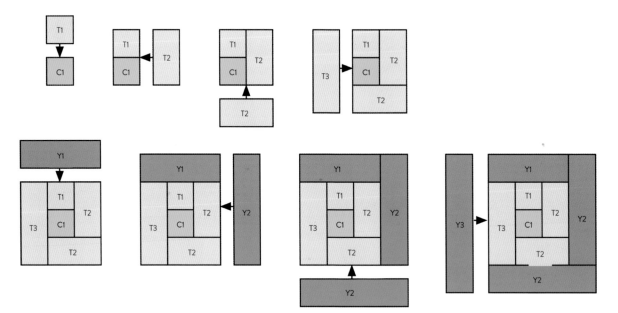

*Step 2.1*

# Step 1: Cut the Fabric

1.  Using your rotary cutter, ruler and cutting mat, cut all your fabric according to the chart on page 33. Set your binding and backing fabric aside for later, along with any leftover fabric.

# Step 2: Assemble the Blocks

1.  This wall hanging is based on the traditional log cabin quilt block. We'll start by learning how to assemble the two and a half blocks that make up the design. The log cabin block starts from the center square and builds outwards, adding a new "log" to each side to make the block larger.

    To assemble Block A, start by sewing C1 to T1 along one side and press your seams open. Then sew T2 to your C1 + T1 along the long edge and press your seams open. Take another T2 and sew the long edge to the C1 + T2 side. Complete that layer by sewing T3 to the remaining open side of C1 and press your seams open. Using the diagram for Block A, continue with these steps, working clockwise and adding the next "log" to each side until the block is complete.

2.  After you've constructed Block A, use the Block B assembly diagram and repeat the same techniques to assemble Block B.

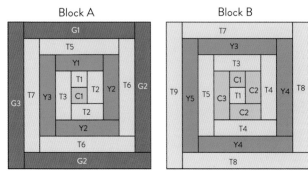

*Step 2.2*

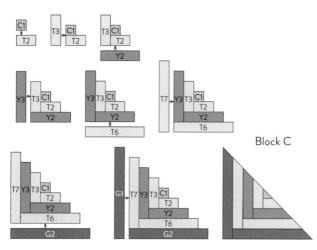

Step 2.3

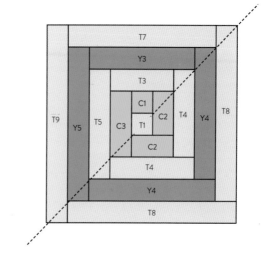

Step 2.4

3. Block C is only a half block. While it uses similar construction methods, follow the diagram above to assemble Block C. Press the seams open. Then place your ruler across the top at the widest point, and trim the ends of the blocks off at an angle so you have a straight edge.

4. When all your blocks are assembled, press all your seams. Then take your ruler and rotary cutter and cut Block B in half diagonally from corner to corner to create Block B1 and Block B2.

## Step 3: Complete the Quilt Top

1. You should have four pieces—Block A, Block B1, Block B2 and Block C. Sew Block B1 onto the left side of Block A. Then sew Block B2 onto the right side of Block C. Press the seams open. Finally, sew these two pieces together along the long edges, making sure your center seams align to ensure your points meet.

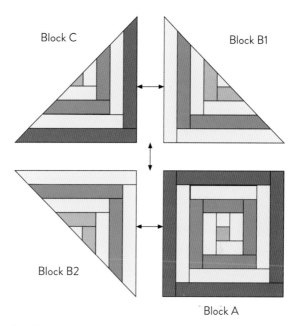

Step 3.1

## Step 4: Finish the Wall Hanging

1.  Following the steps on page 15, press all your seams open, and iron to smooth the quilt top and backing fabric. Baste and quilt using the methods on page 16.

2.  Before binding your wall hanging, cut two 4 x 4" (10.2 x 10.2-cm) squares out of your leftover fabric. These will become the tabs at the top corners to mount your wall hanging. Fold each square in half diagonally, and press at the fold to create two triangles. On the back side of your wall hanging, place each triangle in the top two corners, lining up the corners and the short legs with the edge of the wall hanging. Pin in place. Then sew a scant ¼" (6-mm) seam allowance along the top and side of both triangles. These stitches will be covered by your binding.

3.  Bind following the method on page 24.

4.  To mount your wall hanging, insert a wooden dowel that's 1" (2.5 cm) shorter than the width of your wall hanging. Use one or two nails or a removable adhesive strip to mount on the wall.

*Step 4.2*

## Inspiration

With years of drought under its belt, the hills of California have turned from green to gold. As devastating as the lack of water in California is, the Golden State really lives up to its name, especially during golden hour. The sun lights up the hills, accentuating the yellows, caramels and golds.

With the Atascadero Wall Hanging, named after a small town in central California surrounded by rolling hills, I wanted to use the shape and colors to mimic the gentle peaks and the layers of golden sunshine on the hills. In terms of design, I like to think about wall hangings the way I think about art. Before designing any element of a wall hanging, I ask myself three questions:

• Do I want this to be a statement piece or play a supporting role?

• What colors are going to work well in the space?

• How is the quilting going to accentuate the shape and design of this piece?

THE ABIQUIU CRIB QUILT is a complex design with lots of piecing. By breaking it down into distinct sections, the construction remains straightforward. Using a combination of squares and rectangles creates a dynamic design reminiscent of Navajo weavings and the landscape of northern New Mexico. There's so much going on with the piecing in the Abiquiu Crib Quilt, so I chose to keep the stitching simple with matchstick quilting. This gives the quilt texture and maintains the design's strong vertical lines.

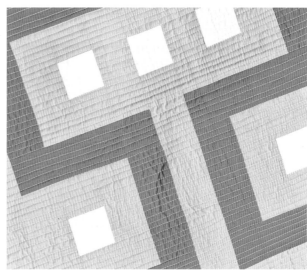

# ABIQUIU CRIB QUILT

38 x 50" (96.5 x 127 cm)

| Fabric | Yardage | # of Pieces | Dimensions | Name |
|---|---|---|---|---|
| Wheat | 1½ yards (1.4 m) | 36 | 2½ x 2½" (6.3 x 6.3 cm) | W1 |
| | | 8 | 4½ x 2½" (11.4 x 6.3 cm) | W2 |
| | | 20 | 6½ x 2½" (16.5 x 6.3 cm) | W3 |
| | | 2 | 8½ x 2½" (21.6 x 6.3 cm) | W4 |
| | | 2 | 14½ x 2½" (36.8 x 6.3 cm) | W5 |
| | | 6 | 50½ x 2½" (128.3 x 6.3 cm) | W6 |
| Sienna | ¾ yard (0.7 m) | 2 | 50½ x 2½" (128.3 x 6.3 cm) | |
| | | 5 | 2½" (6.3 cm) x WOF | Binding |
| Terracotta | ½ yard (0.5 m) | 4 | 4½ x 2½" (11.4 x 6.3 cm) | T1 |
| | | 10 | 6½ x 2½" (16.5 x 6.3 cm) | T2 |
| | | 12 | 8½ x 2½" (21.6 x 6.3 cm) | T3 |
| Peach | ¼ yard (0.2 m) | 4 | 4½ x 2½" (11.4 x 6.3 cm) | P1 |
| | | 10 | 6½ x 2½" (16.5 x 6.3 cm) | P2 |
| Natural | ¼ yard (0.2 m) | 17 | 2½ x 2½" (6.3 x 6.3 cm) | |
| Flax Linen (Yarn Dyed) | 1½ yards (1.4 m) | 1 | 36 x 54" (91.4 x 137.2 cm) | Backing |
| Batting | 42 x 54" (106.7 x 137.12 cm) | | | |

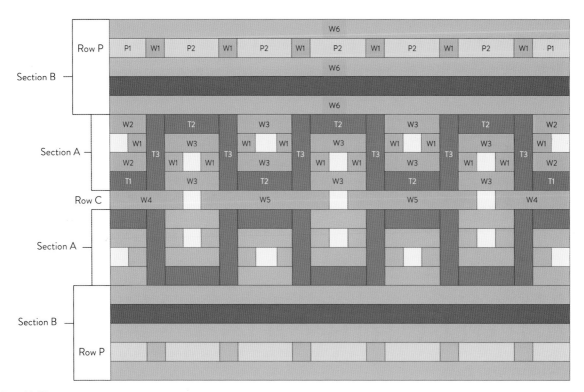

*Assembly Diagram*

## Step 1: Cut the Fabric

1. Cut your fabric according to the chart on page 39. Because all of the pieces in this pattern are 2½" (6.3 cm) wide, it's easiest to cut your fabric into 2½" (6.3-cm) strips and then cut them down into individual pieces.

2. For the Wheat, cut your fabric into 2½" (6.3-cm) strips lengthwise instead of by the WOF in order to get the longest strips without having to sew multiple pieces together. Although for the two long Sienna strips, the fabric allowance requires you to sew an extra piece about 9" (22.9 cm) long onto the end to make it the full 50½" (128.3 cm).

3. Set aside your binding and backing fabric for later, and organize the fabric pieces neatly.

## Step 2: Assemble Section A

1. The most complex part of this quilt top is piecing two identical Section As made up of Block 1, 2 and 3, so let's tackle that first. Start out by sewing your Natural squares and W1 squares together in pairs: Place one Natural square on top of a W1 square. Line up the edges, and sew along the right edge with a ¼" (6-mm) seam allowance. Repeat this with thirteen more Natural squares + W1 squares until you have fourteen total. Press your seams open. Set four of them aside—these will be for Blocks 1 and 2. With the remaining ten Natural + W1's, place a second W1 on top of the Natural square and sew along the opposite edge to make a W1 + Natural + W1 trio for your Block 3s. Press the seams open.

2. To complete your Blocks 1 and 2, take the four Natural + W1 pairs you set aside and sew a W2 rectangle onto the top and bottom of each pair. Press the seams open, then sew a T1 rectangle onto the bottom of two blocks to finish two Block 1s. With the remaining two, sew a T1 rectangle onto the top of the block to finish two Block 2s.

3. For the Block 3s, sew a W3 rectangle onto the top and bottom of your ten W1 + Natural + W1 trios. To finish the Block 3s, take the ten blocks and sew a T2 rectangle onto the bottom of each block to complete ten of Block 3. You should end up with two Block 1s, two Block 2s and ten Block 3s.

4. To assemble Section A, you'll sew these blocks together with a T3 rectangle pieced vertically between each block. Refer to the assembly diagram, making sure the blocks are oriented correctly. Repeat to make two identical Section As. Press all your seams open.

## Step 3: Piece the Rows Together

1. Next you'll put together the Row C and Row P before sewing them to the rest of the strips. Start with the Row P: Sew six W1 squares and five P2 rectangles together, starting and ending each row with a P1 rectangle. Press all your seams open. Repeat to make a second identical Row P.

2. When your Row Ps are complete, sew your W6 and Sienna strips together along the long edges until you have two identical Section Bs.

3. To make Row C, take your remaining three Natural squares along with your W4 and W5 rectangles and sew together.

## Step 4: Complete the Quilt Top

1. To finish assembling your quilt top, you'll sew the two Section As + Row C together and then sew the two Section Bs onto the top and bottom, referring to the assembly diagram for orientation.

2. Start by sewing the Row C between the two Section As along the long edge. Make sure the Natural squares in each section align vertically, pinning to make sure your sections don't shift while sewing.

3. Then sew the long edges of the Section Bs to the top and bottom of Sections A. It can be a little tricky, but try and align the vertical edges of your Peach and Tan rectangles as best you can. This will ensure than your quilting rows are straight and neat.

## Step 5: Finish the Quilt

1. Following the steps on page 15, press all your seams open, and iron to smooth the quilt top and backing fabric. Baste, quilt and bind using your preferred method.

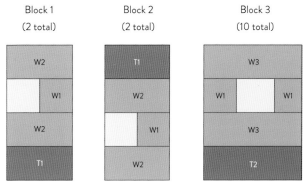

Block 1 (2 total)    Block 2 (2 total)    Block 3 (10 total)

*Step 2.3*

Row P (2 total)

*Step 3.1*

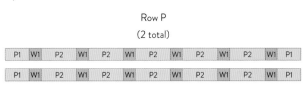

Section B (2 total)

*Step 3.2*

Row C

*Step 3.3*

## Inspiration

Abiquiu is a small town in northern New Mexico where painter Georgia O'Keeffe made her home and found inspiration for her work. After visiting, it was clear why she was so drawn to this place. The ranch where she lived is surrounded by warm, multicolored rock formations and jaw-dropping vistas as far as the eye can see. The design and colors of the Abiquiu Crib Quilt are meant to echo that landscape while giving a slight nod to motifs found in Native American weavings.

THIS THROW-SIZE QUILT, inspired by Antelope Canyon in southern Utah, uses rectangles and a repeating pattern that radiates from the center to create a simple, yet striking, design. I wanted to capture the feeling of walking through the slot canyon by using warm, earthy colors, distilling the narrow undulating walls into a single, repeating rectangular shape, and creating movement with stepped rectangles.

# ANTELOPE CANYON THROW

60 x 60" (152.4 x 152.4 cm)

| Fabric | Yardage | # of Pieces | Dimensions | Name |
|---|---|---|---|---|
| Terracotta | 3¼ yards (3 m) | 4 | 3½ x 6½" (8.9 x 16.5 cm) | T1 |
| | | 8 | 3½ x 9½" (8.9 x 24.1 cm) | T2 |
| | | 8 | 3½ x 18½" (8.9 x 47 cm) | T3 |
| | | 4 | 3½ x 24½" (8.9 x 62.2 cm) | T4 |
| | | 8 | 3½ x 27½" (8.9 x 69.9 cm) | T5 |
| | | 4 | 3½ x 42½" (8.9 x 108 cm) | T6 |
| | | 3 | 6½ x 60½" (16.5 x 153.7 cm) | T7 |
| | | 6 | 2½" (6.3 cm) x WOF | Binding |
| Peach | ½ yard (0.5 m) | 14 | 3½ x 12½" (8.9 x 31.7 cm) | |
| Tan | ½ yard (0.5 m) | 14 | 3½ x 12½" (8.9 x 31.7 cm) | |
| Gold | 3½ yards (3.2 m) | 2 | 64" (162.6 cm) x WOF | Backing |
| Batting | | | 64 x 64" (162.6 x 162.6 cm) | |

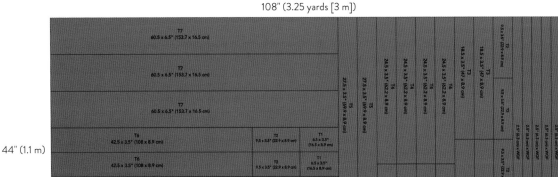

108" (3.25 yards [3 m])

44" (1.1 m)

| T7 60.5 x 6.5" (153.7 x 16.5 cm) |
| T7 60.5 x 6.5" (153.7 x 16.5 cm) |
| T7 60.5 x 6.5" (153.7 x 16.5 cm) |

T6 42.5 x 3.5" (108 x 8.9 cm) | T2 9.5 x 3.5" (22.9 x 8.9 cm) | T1 6.5 x 3.5" (16.5 x 8.9 cm)
T6 42.5 x 3.5" (108 x 8.9 cm) | T2 9.5 x 3.5" (22.9 x 8.9 cm) | T1 6.5 x 3.5" (16.5 x 8.9 cm)
T6 42.5 x 3.5" (108 x 8.9 cm) | T2 9.5 x 3.5" (22.9 x 8.9 cm) | T1 6.5 x 3.5" (16.5 x 8.9 cm)
T6 42.5 x 3.5" (108 x 8.9 cm) | T2 9.5 x 3.5" (22.9 x 8.9 cm) | T1 6.5 x 3.5" (16.5 x 8.9 cm)

T5 27.5 x 3.5" (69.9 x 8.9 cm) | T5 27.5 x 3.5" (69.9 x 8.9 cm)
T5 27.5 x 3.5" (69.9 x 8.9 cm) | T5 27.5 x 3.5" (69.9 x 8.9 cm)
T5 27.5 x 3.5" (69.9 x 8.9 cm) | T5 27.5 x 3.5" (69.9 x 8.9 cm)

*Step 1.1*

Binding
2" (5 cm) x WOF

# Step 1: Cut the Fabric

1. Take full advantage of your yardage by using the chart on page 43 and the diagram above to cut the Terracotta fabric into designated pieces. Set aside your binding for later and stack your pieces by size.

2. For the Peach fabric, cut one 12½" (31.7-cm) x WOF strip then cut into twelve 3½" (8.9-cm) pieces. Cut one 3½" (8.9-cm) x WOF strip then cut into two 12½" (31.7-cm) strips. Repeat the same for the Tan fabric.

3. Cut your Gold backing fabric in half and trim the selvedge off. Set aside for later.

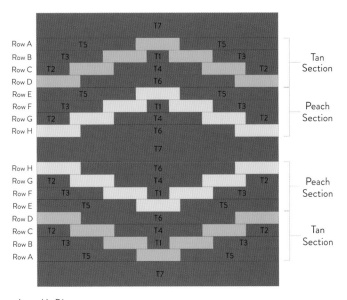

*Assembly Diagram*

*Step 2.2*

*Step 2.3*

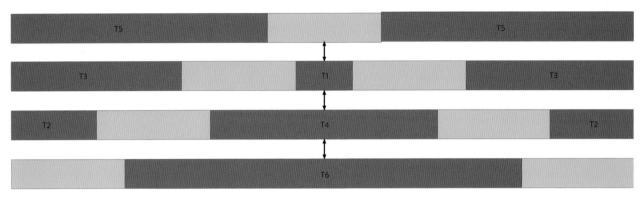

*Step 3.2*

## Step 2: Assemble the Rows

1.  To piece the quilt top together, the first step is assembling the individual rows that make up each section. As you can see in the assembly diagram on page 44, the quilt is made up of four identical sections in two different colors, Peach and Tan. So when assembling your rows, it's quicker and you'll stay more organized if you make two at a time.

2.  Starting with Row A, place one Tan piece on top of one T5 piece, lining up the short edges of the rectangles. Sew along the short edge with a ¼" (6-mm) seam allowance. Unfold the two pieces so the Terracotta is on the left and Tan is on the right.

3.  Take another T5 piece and place it on top of your T5 + Tan piece, lining up the short edge with the open edge of the Tan piece. Sew along the short edge, unfold and press both seams open. You've made your first row! Now repeat the same process to make your second Row A.

4.  Referring to the assembly diagram for the row patterns and piece requirements, repeat the above steps to assemble Rows B through H until you have two of each row. You should end up with sixteen rows in total.

## Step 3: Construct the Sections

1.  When all sixteen rows are assembled, you're ready to construct the four sections that make up the quilt top. When assembling each section, remember to keep your Peach and Tan rows in their separate sections.

2.  To begin constructing your first Tan section, lay out Rows A through D on your workspace as shown above. Place Row B on top of Row A with right sides facing, lining up the short edge on the right and bottom long edge. If it's helpful, pin the rows together to keep the rows from shifting. Sew along the long edge with a ¼" (6-mm) seam allowance, then unfold. Repeat with Rows C and D until you have the first Tan section completed.

3.  Repeat this process to construct another Tan Section. Then with Rows E through H, do the same to construct both Peach sections. You'll end up with four sections.

## Step 4: Complete the Quilt Top

1.  To finish assembling your quilt top, you'll sew the sections together and add in the T7 pieces, referring to the assembly diagram for orientation.

2.  Take one Tan Section and place a Peach Section on top with the right sides facing, so that the bottom of Row D and the top of Row E are lined up. Line up the edges, sew along the long edge with a ¼" (6-mm) seam allowance and unfold. Do the same with your remaining Tan and Peach Section.

3.  Then, place a T7 piece at the top of the Tan Section (where Row A is) with right sides facing, and sew along the long edge. Repeat with another T7 piece on the other Tan Section.

4.  With the final T7 piece, sew onto the open long edge of the Peach Section (where Row H is) and unfold. Then, with right sides facing, sew the open long edge of T7 onto the open long edge of the other Peach Section to complete the quilt top.

## Step 5: Finish the Quilt

1.  Sew the two pieces of backing fabric together along the long edge. Press the seams open. Following the steps on page 15, press all your seams open, and iron to smooth the quilt top and backing fabric. Baste, quilt and bind using your favorite method.

2.  For the Antelope Canyon Throw, I wanted to emphasize the organic curves and shapes of the canyon walls, so I chose to machine quilt slightly wavy lines across the entire quilt to soften the strong, sharp shapes. I used the same Terracotta cotton for the binding so it would disappear and not detract from the design.

## Inspiration

After traveling all over the United States and seeing some of the most beautiful landscapes in the world, Antelope Canyon is, by far, the most impressive natural place I've ever experienced. From the hot desert surface, you descend a staircase into the cool slot canyon. The canyon's tall, undulating walls of warmly colored rock twist and turn to lead you from one "room" to the next. Light streams in beams from above, casting shadows and shifting the colors of these slowly shaped sandstone surfaces. Voices are hushed and everyone is in awe. It feels like being in a place of worship.

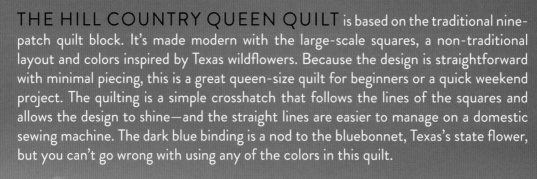

THE HILL COUNTRY QUEEN QUILT is based on the traditional nine-patch quilt block. It's made modern with the large-scale squares, a non-traditional layout and colors inspired by Texas wildflowers. Because the design is straightforward with minimal piecing, this is a great queen-size quilt for beginners or a quick weekend project. The quilting is a simple crosshatch that follows the lines of the squares and allows the design to shine—and the straight lines are easier to manage on a domestic sewing machine. The dark blue binding is a nod to the bluebonnet, Texas's state flower, but you can't go wrong with using any of the colors in this quilt.

# HILL COUNTRY QUEEN QUILT

90 x 90" (228.6 x 228.6 cm)

| Fabric | Yardage | # of Pieces | Dimensions |
|---|---|---|---|
| Natural | 4⅔ yards (4.3 m) | 2 | 90½ x 9½" (229.9 x 24.1 cm) |
| | | 2 | 72½ x 9½" (184.2 x 24.1 cm) |
| | | 46 | 8½ x 8½" (21.6 x 21.6 cm) |
| Cayenne | ½ yard (0.5 m) | 8 | 8½ x 8½" (21.6 x 21.6 cm) |
| Sienna | ¼ yard (0.25 m) | 5 | 8½ x 8½" (21.6 x 21.6 cm) |
| Dark Blue | 1¼ yard (1.2 m) | 8 | 8½ x 8½" (21.6 x 21.6 cm) |
| | | 9 | 2½" (6.3 cm) x WOF |
| Medium Blue | ¾ yard (0.7 m) | 12 | 8½ x 8½" (21.6 x 21.6 cm) |
| Indigo Linen (Yarn Dyed) | 5¼ yards (4.8 m) | 2 | 94" (238.8 cm) x WOF |
| Batting | 96 x 96" (243.8 x 243.8 cm) | | |

## Step 1: Cut the Fabric

1. Cut your fabric based on the chart on page 49. Because this pattern is mostly 8½" (21.6-cm) squares you can get five 8½" (21.6-cm) squares from your fabric's 44" (111.8-cm) width. Cut one 8½" (21.6-cm) strip of Sienna, two strips of Cayenne, two strips of Dark Blue and three strips of Medium Blue before cutting those into individual 8½" (21.6-cm) squares.

2. For your Natural fabric, cut a piece that's 90½" (229.9 cm) x WOF and then cut your long strips from the length of that piece. Then use the method above to cut 8½" (21.6-cm) strips, then individual 8½" (21.6-cm) squares from the remaining fabric.

3. Cut your Indigo fabric in half, and trim selvedge off. Set aside with the 2½" (6.3-cm) strips of Dark Blue fabric and whatever leftover fabric you have for later.

## Step 2: Assemble the Blocks

1. This pattern is based on the traditional nine-patch quilt block, with three unique nine-patch blocks in this design.

> Note: Try chain piecing with this pattern! You're making a lot of the same blocks, so chain piecing (page 58) will make repetitive piecing like this much more efficient.

2. Starting with Row A, stack two Natural squares and sew along the right edge. Repeat until you have eight total. Open up the two pieces, place a Cayenne square on top of the Natural square on the left, line up the edges and sew along the left edge. Repeat until you have eight of Row A.

3. Referring to the assembly diagram for the row patterns and piece requirements, repeat the steps to assemble Rows B through D, and press all your seams open. You should end up with 8 Row As, 8 Row Cs, 5 Row Bs and 6 Row Ds.

4. After your rows are made, it's time to assemble the blocks. Starting with the Red Block, sew Row B to the bottom long edge of Row A. Then flip a second Row A around so the Cayenne square is on the right and sew the second Row A to the bottom long edge of Row B. Make sure to line up your seams so the corners of each square meet perfectly at the corners. Repeat to make three more Red Blocks (four total). Then, using the same method and the diagrams, make four Blue Blocks and one Central Block. Press all your seams open.

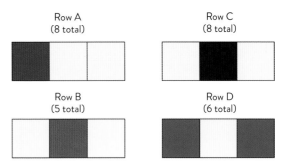

Row A (8 total)  Row C (8 total)

Row B (5 total)  Row D (6 total)

*Step 2.3*

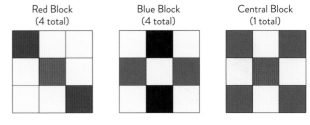

Red Block (4 total)  Blue Block (4 total)  Central Block (1 total)

*Step 2.4*

## Step 3: Assemble the Quilt Top

1. Using the diagram, assemble your nine blocks together by row, taking extra care to line up your seams and paying attention to the orientation of the blocks. When assembling larger blocks that have multiple seams that need to line up, I use straight pins at each seam to hold the layers of fabric in place and to keep them from shifting. When you sew the three rows together, sew those rows together along the long edges.

2. After you've sewn all nine blocks together, you're ready to add the border to finish your quilt top. Sew the 72½" (184.2-cm) long Natural strips to the right and left sides of the quilt top. Then sew the 90½" (229.9-cm) long Natural strips onto the top and bottom of your quilt top.

## Step 4: Finish the Quilt

1. Sew your scraps together into a strip that's 94" (238.8 cm) long and at least 8" (20.3 cm) wide. Then sew the two pieces of backing fabric to either side of your scrap strip along the long edge. Press the seams open.

2. Following the steps outlined on page 15, press all your seams open, and iron to smooth the quilt top and backing fabric. Baste, quilt and bind using your favorite method.

## Inspiration

Growing up in Texas, springtime road trips through the Hill Country to visit my grandparents meant watching the miles and miles of roadside covered in bluebonnets and Indian paint brushes. Blankets of these wildflowers cover most medians and fields across the state every spring—it's truly a sight to see. With a traditional design reminiscent of the small sweet Texas towns we'd drive through, the colors of wildflowers are scattered across the quilt, just like they are in the roadside fields.

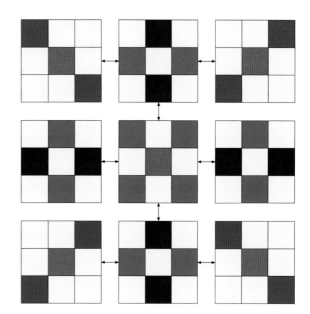

Step 3.1

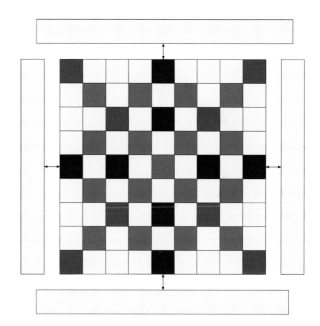

Step 3.2

# DESIGN NOTES

## Distilling Design

The secret to designing a simple geometric quilt is to keep your shapes simple. There are only a few basic shapes I use in this book: squares, rectangles, triangles and curves. It's amazing how many ways you can combine, rotate and repeat those shapes to make some unique and incredible quilt patterns. And less is more in terms of quantity. If you find yourself in the middle of a design and it feels too busy, take something (or a few things) away and see if it works better. Negative space is your friend when it comes to keeping your designs minimal.

If I'm taking inspiration from a photograph or a location, I like to take the main features that stand out to me and figure out which shape would represent that feature best. Let's take the Tent Rocks Pillow (page 123). I wanted to highlight the pointy rock formations that give Tent Rocks its name, and it seemed obvious to me that the shape should be an elongated triangle. To balance out that long pointed shape, a curved half circle to represent the warm New Mexico sun sits on the opposite side. Choosing to do three "tent rocks" created the right balance in number and size. The negative space of the background speaks for itself and allows those simple shapes to shine.

I've always found that sketching a lot of different iterations of the same design can help you find the best one. Sometimes it just takes erasing one line or turning a triangle the other way to really make a design pop. Don't get frustrated if your design isn't finding its groove: I've sketched hundreds of designs that just didn't work no matter how many times I tried. Taking some space and stepping away for a few days (or a few months!) can be helpful until you figure out the best solution for your design.

TENT ROCKS

Mixing It
Up with Versatile
Triangles

TRIANGLES, specifically half square triangles (HSTs) and half rectangle triangles (HRTs), are one of the most versatile shapes to use in your quilts. There are endless combinations, patterns and designs that can be created from triangles alone. When you learn the technique for making HSTs and HRTs, it'll be hard to get bored with them because of how much you can do.

What I love so much about using triangles in my quilts is how the same shape can be both traditional and modern depending on the colors and the pattern. The Minnesota Throw Quilt (page 75) recalls classic quilt patterns, but with its large-scale piecing and high-contrast colors, it doesn't look old fashioned. The Pescadero Crib Quilt (page 71) combines HSTs and HRTs to create an unexpected, modern design that's timeless.

Triangles are my favorite shape to use for conveying energy and motion. The direction of the HSTs in the New Mexico Queen Quilt (page 81) make for a dynamic flow of energy across the quilt, while the columns of triangles in the Montara Wall Hanging (page 67) evoke the repetitive motion of waves crashing on the beach.

Working through the projects in this section, you'll learn the techniques for making HSTs and HRTs, and how to assemble them into a cohesive quilt, pillow or wall hanging. I share a few tricks of the trade to work more efficiently and piece more accurately, and I let you in on a couple design secrets.

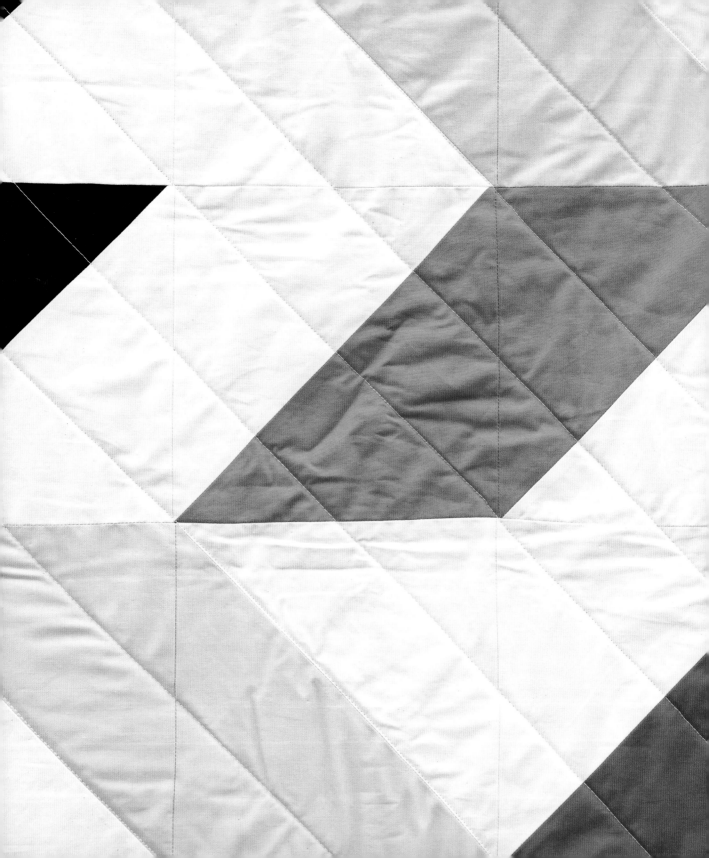

# TECHNIQUE TUTORIAL

## Half Square Triangles and Half Rectangle Triangles

In this chapter, all five projects will be based on half square triangles (HSTs) and half rectangle triangles (HRTs). The steps below detail the foundational techniques for both.

## Half Square Triangles (HSTs)

The easiest and most efficient way I've found to make HSTs is the two-at-a-time method, where you make two HSTs at once from two squares of fabric.

The general rule for determining the size of the squares you start with is to take your finished HST dimensions (without the seam allowance included) and add ⅞" (2.2 cm). To make sure I have enough wiggle room, I prefer to add 1" (2.5 cm) and trim my HSTs down. So if you want your finished HSTs to be 3 x 3" (7.6 x 7.6 cm) or 3½ x 3½" (8.9 x 8.9 cm) including seam allowance, I'd cut two 4 x 4" (10.2 x 10.2-cm) squares.

Start by marking a crease diagonally from corner to corner on one of your squares with a fabric marker. Then, place that square directly on top of the second square, lining up the edges and pinning on either side of the crease.

Sew down the left side of the crease with a ¼" (6-mm) seam allowance, using the right edge of your presser foot as a guide. When you reach the end of the square, flip the square around to sew along the opposite side of the crease with a ¼" (6-mm) seam allowance.

*Half square triangles and half rectangle triangles are simple shapes with a lot of versatility.*

*Place one square on top of the other.*

*Sew ¼" (6 mm) to the left of the center crease.*

*Cut along the center crease.*

When the square has been sewn on both sides of the crease, use your ruler and rotary cutter to cut along the crease, separating your squares into two individual pieces. Unfold each HST, press the seams open, and trim both squares down to 3½ x 3½" (8.9 x 8.9 cm).

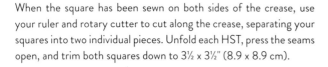

Tip: If you're making many HSTs, try chain piecing! After you sew the first side of your first squares, instead of flipping it around to sew along the opposite side, just begin sewing the next squares along the same side without breaking your thread. Continue until all your squares are sewn on the same side. This creates a "chain" of squares all connected by the same thread. When you get to the end, turn your chain of squares around and sew along the other side of the crease, repeating for the rest of them. When you're finished, snip the threads connecting each square and stack neatly.

## Half Rectangle Triangles (HRTs)

Making half rectangle triangles is a bit different than making HSTs. I learned the hard way that if you try making them the same way, you'll end up with two kite-shaped blocks.

To determine the dimensions of your starting rectangles, I add ¼" (6 mm) to the width of my block including the seam allowance and ½" (12 mm) to the length of my block including the seam allowance.

Start by stacking your two rectangles, and cut both diagonally from top left corner to bottom right corner. Keep in mind that, unlike HSTs that can be rotated any way, the diagonal you cut on can only be rotated two ways. You'll end up with four triangles.

*Sew the HRT down the longest edge.*

Then place one triangle from each rectangle on top of one together with right sides facing and the skinny points overlapping by ¼" (6 mm), lining up the longest edge. Sew them together along the long edge with a ¼" (6-mm) seam allowance and press the seam open. Trim your HRT down to the proper dimensions.

▶ ◀
▶ Note: It's important to trim all your HSTs and HRTs ◀
▶ so they're identical and the corners are perfectly ◀
▶ squared. This will ensure your points and seams line ◀
▶ up when you're piecing. ◀

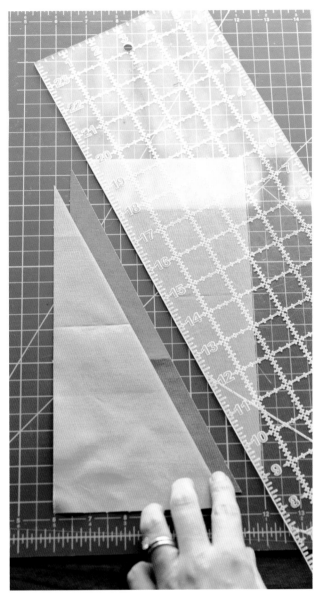
*Stack the rectangles and cut diagonally.*

# WHEN I FIRST DESIGNED THE LONE PINE PILLOW,

I thought it might look so much like a mountain that it would be too kitschy. But by distilling the shapes into the most simple, geometric forms and creating a strong sense of symmetry, there's enough abstraction to make this pattern modern and versatile. So many color palettes would look amazing—you could really make this pattern your own. The smaller fabric requirements make this one a great way to use up scraps.

# LONE PINE PILLOW

18 x 18" (45.7 x 45.7 cm)

| Fabric | Yardage | # of Pieces | Dimensions |
|---|---|---|---|
| Natural | ⅛ yard (0.1 m) | 5 | 4½ x 4½" (11.4 x 11.4 cm) |
| Steel Linen (Yarn Dyed) | ¾ yard (0.7 m) | 2 | 4½ x 4½" (11.4 x 11.4 cm) |
| | | 2 | 18½ x 14" (47 x 35.6 cm) |
| Charcoal | ⅛ yard (0.1 m) | 3 | 4½ x 4½" (11.4 x 11.4 cm) |
| Fog | ¼ yard (0.2 m) | 1 | 9 x 9" (22.9 x 22.9 cm) |
| | | 2 | 2 x 8½" (5 x 21.6 cm) |
| | | 1 | 2 x 19" (5 x 48.3 cm) |
| Army Green | ¼ yard (0.2 m) | 1 | 9 x 9" (22.9 x 22.9 cm) |
| | | 2 | 2 x 8½" (5 x 21.6 cm) |
| | | 1 | 2 x 19" (5 x 48.3 cm) |
| Batting | 20 x 20" (50.8 x 50.8 cm) | | |
| Pillow Insert | 20 x 20" (50.8 x 50.8 cm) | | |

## Step 1: Cut the Fabric

1. Using your rotary cutter, ruler and cutting mat, cut all your fabric according to the chart on page 61. Set the two 18½ x 14" (47 x 35.6-cm) Steel rectangles aside for assembling the pillow back later.

## Step 2: Make the Half Square Triangles (HSTs)

1. Start by making all your half square triangles. For detailed photos and tips on making two-at-a-time HSTs, refer to the Technique Tutorial (page 57).

2. Take the five 4½" (11.4-cm) Natural squares and mark a crease diagonally from corner to corner. Place each square on top of the other 4½" (11.4-cm) Steel and Charcoal squares you cut, lining up the edges and pinning on either side of the crease. Then you'll sew ¼" (6 mm) to the left of the crease, using the edge of your presser foot as a guide. When you reach the end of the square, flip your square around and sew along the opposite side of the crease. Repeat with all your squares.

3. When all your squares have been sewn on both sides of the crease, use your ruler and rotary cutter to cut along each crease. Discard one of your Steel HSTs and you should end up with three Steel HSTs and six Charcoal HSTs. Press your seams open before trimming each square down to 4 x 4" (10.2 x 10.2 cm).

## Step 3: Assemble the HSTs

1. For the HST block, you'll sew your HSTs together in rows of three, then sew each row together. Using the diagram for the pattern and orientation, sew the following:

   • Top Row: two Steel + one Charcoal

   • Middle Row: one Steel + two Charcoal

   • Bottom Row: three Charcoal

2. When sewing your rows together, take extra care to align the seams to ensure your triangle points meet. Press all your seams open.

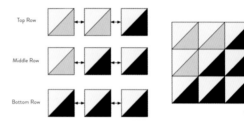

*Step 3.1*

# Step 4: Complete the Pillow Top

1.  Start by taking your two 9" (22.9-cm) Fog and Army Green squares and cut each one in half diagonally. Take one of the Fog half squares and place it on the HST block with right sides facing, lining up the top side of the block with the long edge of the Fog half square. The two points of the Fog half square should stick out about 1" (2.5 cm) past the HST block on both sides. Sew along the top edge with a ¼" (6-mm) seam allowance, being careful not to stretch the fabric of the Fog half square. Press the seam open. With the remaining Fog half square, repeat the steps above, sewing the half square to the left side of the block, making sure to center the half square on the HST block. The points of the Fog half squares should overlap.

2.  Following the same steps, sew your Army Green half squares to the right side and bottom sides of your HST block. Press all your seams open. Place your ruler ¼" (6 mm) past the corners of the HST block and trim your new block down so that there's a ¼" (6-mm) border around the HST block.

3.  To complete your pillow top, take all four of your 8½" (21.6-cm) strips and sew one Fog strip to one Army Green strip along the short end. Repeat to make two identical pairs and press the seams open. Then you'll sew these pairs onto the left and right sides of your block, making sure the colors are on the correct side (Fog on top, Army Green on bottom) and align the center seam of your strip with the point of your HST block. Press those seams open, and trim the ends of the strips if they extend past the block.

4.  Finally, sew the 19" (48.3-cm) Fog strip to the top edge of the block and the 19" (48.3-cm) Army Green strip to the bottom. Press all your seams open to complete your pillow top.

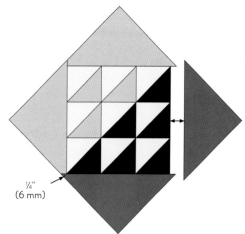

¼"
(6 mm)

Step 4.2

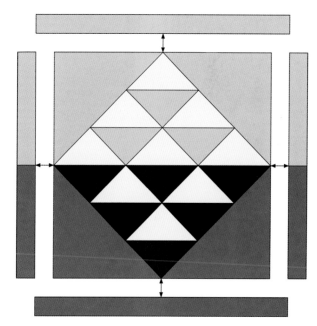

Step 4.3

## Step 5: Finish the Pillow

1.  Press all your seams open, and iron to smooth the pillow top and backing fabric. The backing fabric will be on the inside of the pillow, so feel free to use any 20 x 20" (50.8 x 50.8-cm) piece of fabric you have. Following the steps on page 16, baste and quilt using your favorite method, then trim your top down to 18½ x 18½" (47 x 47 cm).

2.  Take the two 18½ x 14" (47 x 35.5-cm) steel fabric pieces and hem each piece along the longest edge. To do that, fold the edge over ½" (12 mm) and press flat. Then fold another ½" (12 mm) and press. Sew along the edge of your first fold, securing the hem.

3.  Next, place your pillow on your workspace with the right side facing up. Take one of your hemmed backing pieces and place it on top with the right side (the smooth side of the hem) facing down. Line up the raw long edge with the top and sides of your pillow top. Do the same with your other backing piece, but align the long raw edge with the bottom of the pillow top. Your two backing pieces should overlap by a few inches. Pin around the edges, and sew with a ¼" (6-mm) seam allowance all the way around the square. Then trim the corners at an angle to reduce bulk, and turn your pillow right side out. Stuff with a 20 x 20" (50.8 x 50.8-cm) pillow insert and you're done!

## Inspiration

Lone Pine sits on the eastern side of the Sierra Nevadas at the base of Mount Whitney, the tallest peak in the lower 48 states. My husband and I camped in the foothills the week of Thanksgiving, when the temperatures were in the teens and the wind was brutal. It was pretty miserable. But waking up to this 14,500-foot (4,420-m) mountain right outside our window with a fresh dusting of snow every morning was humbling and awe-inspiring. The Lone Pine Pillow abstracts the mountain, rising up above the tree line, freshly covered in snow.

**THE MONTARA WALL HANGING** uses the classic half square triangle block to represent the crashing waves and the calming colors of the beach. I loved the idea of quilting around the triangles in the Montara Wall Hanging to accentuate the coastal colors and also create a textural pattern that continues beyond the triangles. With smaller pieces such as wall hangings, it's fun to get creative with the quilting and try out some new techniques!

# MONTARA WALL HANGING

12 x 16" (30.5 x 40.6 cm)

| Fabric | Yardage | # of Pieces | Dimensions |
|---|---|---|---|
| Natural | ⅔ yard (0.6 m) | 12 | 3 x 3" (7.6 x 7.6 cm) |
| | | 4 | 2½ x 12½" (6.3 x 31.7 cm) |
| | | 2 | 2½" (6.3 cm) x WOF |
| | | 1 | 14 x 18" (35.6 x 45.7 cm) |
| Dark Blue | ⅛ yard (0.1 m) | 3 | 3 x 3" (7.6 x 7.6 cm) |
| Medium Blue | ⅛ yard (0.1 m) | 3 | 3 x 3" (7.6 x 7.6 cm) |
| Fog | ⅛ yard (0.1 m) | 3 | 3 x 3" (7.6 x 7.6 cm) |
| Wheat | ⅛ yard (0.1 m) | 3 | 3 x 3" (7.6 x 7.6 cm) |
| Batting | 16 x 20" (40.6 x 50.8 cm) | | |

## Step 1: Cut the Fabric

1. Using your rotary cutter, ruler and cutting mat, cut all your fabric according to the chart on page 67. Set the 2½" (6.3-cm) Natural strips and 14 x 18" (35.6 x 45.7-cm) Natural rectangle aside for the binding and backing along with your leftover fabric.

## Step 2: Make the Half Square Triangles (HSTs)

1. Start by making all your half square triangles. For detailed photos and tips on making two-at-a-time HSTs, refer to the Technique Tutorial (page 57). Take your twelve 3" (7.6-cm) Natural squares and mark a crease diagonally from corner to corner. Place each square on top of the other 3" (7.6-cm) squares you cut, lining up the edges and pinning on either side of the crease. Then you'll sew ¼" (6 mm) to the left of the crease, using the edge of your presser foot as a guide. When you reach the end of the square, flip your square around and sew along the opposite side of the crease. Repeat with all your squares.

2. When all your squares have been sewn on both sides of the crease, use your ruler and rotary cutter to cut along each crease. You should end up with 24 HSTs and six of each color. Press your seams open before trimming each square down to 2½ x 2½" (6.3 x 6.3 cm).

## Step 3: Assemble the HST Columns

1. Next, you'll create four columns of each color and then sew those four columns together. Starting with your Medium Blue HSTs, sew all six into a column, making sure they're all oriented the same way with the corner of the Medium Blue triangle at the bottom left. Do the same with your Wheat HSTs.

2. Repeat the steps above with your Dark Blue and Fog HSTs, but make sure to orient them so the corner of the Dark Blue and Fog triangles are at the bottom right. When all your columns are sewn together, press all your seams open.

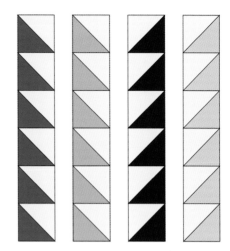

*Step 3.1–3.2*

## Inspiration

Montara Beach, a few miles south of San Francisco, was one of my favorite beaches to visit when I lived nearby. Wide and long, surrounded by steep, succulent-covered cliffs, never crowded and always with rough surf. It was the perfect beach to just sit and watch the ocean. Not to mention, it makes a great backdrop for a quilt!

## Step 4: Complete the Quilt Top

1. To finish making your wall hanging top, sew the columns together according to the diagram, making sure to align the horizontal seams between the HSTs as you go so your triangle points meet. Then sew the 12½" (31.7-cm) Natural strips onto the left and right sides of your HST block. Press the seams open, and then sew the remaining Natural strips onto the top and bottom to complete your quilt top.

## Step 5: Finish the Wall Hanging

1. Following the steps on page 15, press all your seams open, and iron to smooth the quilt top and backing fabric. Baste and quilt using your favorite method.

2. Before binding your wall hanging, cut two 4 x 4" (10.2 x 10.2-cm) squares out of the leftover fabric—these will become the tabs at the top corners to mount your wall hanging. Fold each square in half diagonally and press at the fold to create two triangles. On the back side of your wall hanging, place each triangle in the top two corners, lining up the corners and the short legs with the edge of the wall hanging. Pin in place. Then sew a scant ¼" (6-mm) seam allowance along the top and side of both triangles. These stitches will be covered by your binding.

3. Bind following the method on page 24.

4. To mount your wall hanging, insert a wooden dowel that's 1" (2.5 cm) shorter than the width of your wall hanging. Use one or two nails or a removable adhesive strip to mount on the wall.

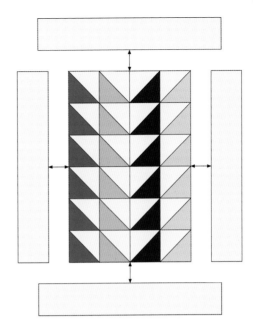

Step 4.1

Step 5.2

**THE PESCADERO CRIB QUILT** takes the organic shape and pattern of mussel shells clustered at low tide and simplifies them, creating order from chaos and a minimal, modern crib quilt. I love working with HSTs and HRTs together—they create such a dynamic sense of movement, and there are endless ways of combining them to make new designs. The clusters of mussels that inspired the design inform the diagonal quilting, which creates connection between each triangle and represents the constant movement of the ocean.

# PESCADERO CRIB QUILT

38 x 48" (96.5 x 121.9 cm)

| Fabric | Yardage | # of Pieces | Dimensions |
|---|---|---|---|
| Seafoam | 1¼ yards (1.2 m) | 6 | 8 x 3" (20.3 x 7.6 cm) |
| | | 6 | 13 x 3" (33 x 7.6 cm) |
| | | 3 | 38½ x 3" (97.8 x 7.6 cm) |
| | | 4 | 8½ x 8½" (21.6 x 21.6 cm) |
| | | 4 | 8¼ x 13½" (20.9 x 34.3 cm) |
| Natural | ½ yard (0.5 m) | 2 | 8½ x 8½" (21.6 x 21.6 cm) |
| | | 2 | 8¼ x 13½" (20.9 x 34.3 cm) |
| Dark Blue | ¼ yard (0.2 m) | 2 | 8¼ x 13½" (20.9 x 34.3 cm) |
| Navy | ¾ yard (0.7 m) | 2 | 8½ x 8½" (21.6 x 21.6 cm) |
| | | 5 | 2½" (6.3 cm) x WOF |
| Steel Linen (Yarn Dyed) | 1½ yards (1.4 m) | | |
| Batting | 42 x 52" (106.7 x 132.1 cm) | | |

## Step 1: Cut the Fabric

1. Using your rotary cutter, ruler and cutting mat, cut all your fabric according to the chart on page 71. Set your 2½" (6.3-cm) Navy strips and Steel fabric aside for binding and backing later.

## Step 2: Make the Half Square Triangles (HSTs)

1. Start by making your half square triangles. For detailed photos and tips on making two-at-a-time HSTs, refer to the Technique Tutorial (page 57). Take your four 8½" (21.6-cm) Seafoam squares and mark a crease diagonally from corner to corner. Place each square on top of the other 8½" (21.6-cm) squares you cut, two Natural and two Navy, lining up the edges and pinning on either side of the crease. Then you'll sew ¼" (6 mm) to the left of the crease, using the edge of your presser foot as a guide. When you reach the end of the square, flip your square around and sew along the opposite side of the crease. Repeat with your remaining squares.

2. When all your squares have been sewn on both sides of the crease, use your ruler and rotary cutter to cut along each crease. Press your seams open before trimming each square down to 8 x 8" (20.3 x 20.3 cm).

## Step 3: Make the Half Rectangle Triangles (HRTs)

1. Next, you'll make your half rectangle triangles. Refer to the Technique Tutorial (page 57) for detailed steps, photos and helpful tips on how to make HRTs. Start by cutting your 8¼ x 13½" (20.9 x 34.3-cm) Seafoam, Natural and Dark Blue rectangles diagonally from top left to bottom right corner. Then take one Dark Blue triangle (90-degree corner at the bottom left) and one Seafoam triangle (90-degree corner at the top right) and flip the Seafoam triangle on top of the Dark Blue so right sides are facing and the long edges align. The points should overlap by ¼" (6 mm). Sew along the longest edge with a ¼" (6-mm) seam allowance, then press the seam open.

2. Repeat to make three more identical HRTs, four total. Then with the Natural and Seafoam triangles, follow the same steps above to make four more HRTs. Press all your seams open, and trim each rectangle down to 8 x 13" (20.3 x 33 cm).

## Step 4: Assemble the Rows + Complete the Quilt Top

1. Take your completed HSTs and, starting with a Natural HST and alternating colors, sew two Natural + two Navy HSTs together with a 8 x 3" (20.3 x 7.6-cm) Seafoam rectangle between each HST. Make sure to keep them oriented the same way. Repeat to make two identical rows, and press the seams open.

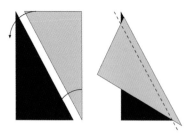

Piecing HRTs

*Step 3.1*

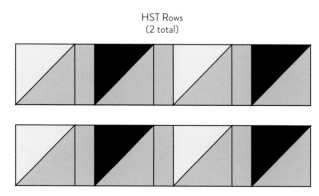

HST Rows
(2 total)

*Step 4.1*

HRT Rows
(2 total)

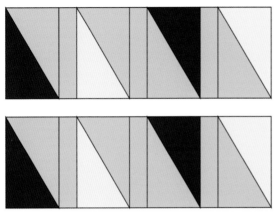

*Step 4.2*

2. Do the same with your HRTs and your 3 x 13" (7.6 x 33-cm) Seafoam rectangles (but start with a Navy HRT), creating two identical rows. Press all your seams open.

3. When your four rows are complete, sew them together along the long edges with a 3 x 38½" (7.6 x 97.8-cm) Seafoam strip between each row. Make sure to orient them according to the assembly diagram opposite.

## Step 5: Finish the Quilt

1. Following the steps on page 15, press all your seams open, and iron to smooth the quilt top and Steel backing fabric. Baste, quilt and bind using your favorite method.

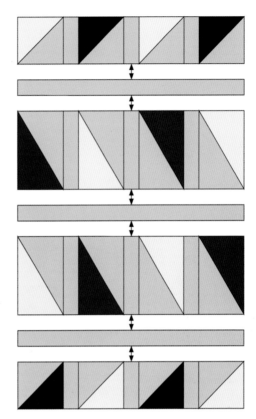

*Step 4.3*

## Inspiration

Pescadero is a small coastal village on California's Slow Coast that runs between Santa Cruz and San Francisco. The beaches in the area are wild, rocky and beautiful—some of my favorite in the country. During low tide, you can hop between the tide pools and see the mussels clustered together on weathered rocks, creating organic shapes that look like they're meant to be. These mussel clusters were the starting point for the seemingly random, but orderly pattern of the Pescadero Crib Quilt.

WITH THE MINNESOTA THROW, I didn't want to capture the look of a place, but more the spirit of it. It's refreshingly simple and makes an impactful statement without needing too much extra. I love the different shapes the triangles create in this design. They turn the negative space into something new, making this simple design incredibly dynamic. I wanted to continue and echo the shapes of the Minnesota Throw in the quilting, especially because there's so much negative space. The radiating V design creates texture and movement within this minimal, large-scale quilt.

# MINNESOTA THROW QUILT

63 x 63" (160 x 160 cm)

| Fabric | Yardage | # of Pieces | Dimensions |
|---|---|---|---|
| Charcoal | 2⅔ yards (2.5 m) | 2 | 63½ x 4" (161.3 x 10.2 cm) |
| | | 2 | 56½ x 4" (143.5 x 10.2 cm) |
| | | 4 | 7½ x 7½" (19 x 19 cm) |
| | | 8 | 14½ x 7½" (36.8 x 19 cm) |
| | | 1 | 14½ x 14½" (36.8 x 36.8 cm) |
| | | 12 | 8 x 8" (20.3 x 20.3 cm) |
| | | 2 | 15 x 15" (38.1 x 38.1 cm) |
| Natural | ¾ yard (0.7 m) | 12 | 8 x 8" (20.3 x 20.3 cm) |
| Terracotta | ½ yard (0.5 m) | 2 | 15 x 15" (38.1 x 38.1 cm) |
| Indigo Linen (Homespun) | 3⅔ yards (3.4 m) | 2 | 66" (167.6 cm) x WOF |
| | | 5 | 66 x 2½" (167.6 x 6.3 cm) |
| Batting | | 67 x 67" (170.2 x 170.2 cm) | |

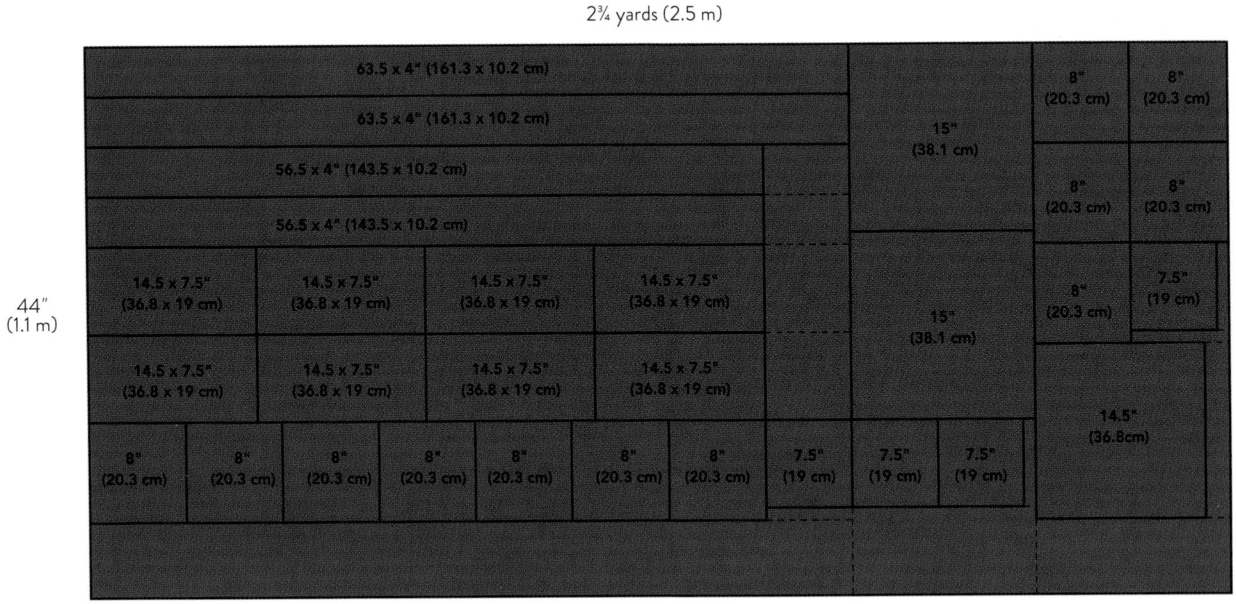

## Step 1.1

2¾ yards (2.5 m)

| 63.5 x 4" (161.3 x 10.2 cm) | | | | | | | | | | 8" (20.3 cm) | 8" (20.3 cm) |

63.5 x 4" (161.3 x 10.2 cm)

15" (38.1 cm)

63.5 x 4" (161.3 x 10.2 cm)

56.5 x 4" (143.5 x 10.2 cm)

8" (20.3 cm) · 8" (20.3 cm)

56.5 x 4" (143.5 x 10.2 cm)

44" (1.1 m)

14.5 x 7.5" (36.8 x 19 cm) · 14.5 x 7.5" (36.8 x 19 cm) · 14.5 x 7.5" (36.8 x 19 cm) · 14.5 x 7.5" (36.8 x 19 cm)

15" (38.1 cm)

8" (20.3 cm) · 7.5" (19 cm)

14.5 x 7.5" (36.8 x 19 cm) · 14.5 x 7.5" (36.8 x 19 cm) · 14.5 x 7.5" (36.8 x 19 cm) · 14.5 x 7.5" (36.8 x 19 cm)

14.5" (36.8cm)

8" (20.3 cm) · 8" (20.3 cm) · 8" (20.3 cm) · 8" (20.3 cm) · 8" (20.3 cm) · 8" (20.3 cm) · 8" (20.3 cm) · 7.5" (19 cm) · 7.5" (19 cm) · 7.5" (19 cm)

## Step 1: Cut the Fabric

1. To make the most of your Charcoal fabric, cut according to the diagram above. Cut the Natural and Terracotta fabric based on the chart on page 75.

2. Cut the Indigo fabric into two pieces, then cut five 2½ x 66" (6.3 x 167.6 cm) strips from one of those pieces. Set aside for the backing and binding.

## Step 2: Make the Half Square Triangles (HSTs)

1. Start by making your half square triangles. For detailed photos and tips on making two-at-a-time HSTs, refer to the Technique Tutorial (page 57). This pattern calls for 24 Charcoal and Natural HSTs and 4 large Charcoal and Terracotta HSTs. So take your 8" (20.3-cm) and 15" (38.1-cm) Charcoal squares, and mark a crease diagonally from corner to corner. Then place each square on top of a Natural or Terracotta square of the same size, lining up the edges, and pin on either side of the crease. Repeat until all the squares are matched. You should have twelve 8" (20.3-cm) pairs and two 15" (38.1-cm) pairs.

2. Then, you'll sew ¼" (6 mm) to the left of the crease, using the edge of your presser foot as a guide. Because you're sewing so many HSTs at once, I'd recommend chain piecing. That means that once you've sewn the first square, pause for a moment without breaking your thread to grab the next square and feed it through you machine with that same ¼" (6 mm) left of the crease. Continue until you've sewn to the left side of the crease on all your squares. At the end, flip your chain of squares around and stitch along the other side of the crease.

3. When all your squares have been sewn on both sides of the crease, snip the threads connecting each square. Then, using your ruler and rotary cutter, cut along each crease. You'll want to press your seams open before trimming each square down to 7½" (19 cm) and 14½" (36.8 cm) respectively.

## Step 3: Assemble the Quilt Top

1. Start out by sewing your 7½" (19-cm) HSTs into pairs: eight of Pair A and four of Pair B. Then take four of Pair A and sew a 7½" (19-cm) Charcoal square onto the left side of the pair to create four of Trio C.

2. Next, you'll assemble the two main blocks that make up the quilt: Block A and Block B. To assemble Block A, you'll sew Pair A onto the left side of your large Terracotta HST first, press the seams open, then sew Trio C onto the top side of the Pair A + Terracotta HST. Repeat these steps to create four Block As. Then for Block B, sew two 14½ x 7½" (36.8 x 19-cm) Charcoal rectangles onto the top and bottom sides of Pair B. Repeat until you have four Block Bs. Press the seams open.

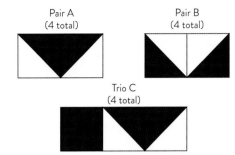

*Step 3.1*

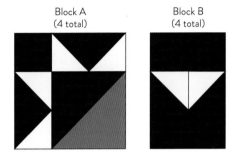

*Step 3.2*

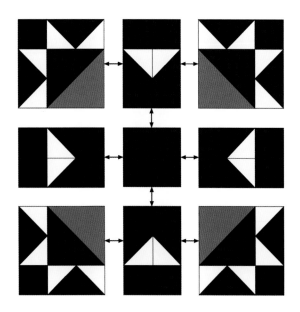

Step 3.3

Step 3.4

3.  To complete your quilt top, sew Block A, Block B, and another Block A together according to the diagram above, making sure to line up your seams. Repeat to make another identical Block A, Block B, plus Block A section. Next, rotate your remaining Block Bs and sew onto each side of the 14½" (36.8-cm) Charcoal square. Press all your seams open.

4.  Sew the three sections together, making sure to line up your seams, then attach both 56½" (143.5-cm) Charcoal strips to the right and left side and both 63½" (161.3-cm) Charcoal strips to the top and bottom to finish your Minnesota Quilt top.

## Step 4: Finish the Quilt

1.  Sew the two pieces of Indigo fabric together along the long edge. Press the seams open. Following the steps on page 15, press all your seams open, and iron to smooth the quilt top and backing fabric. Baste, quilt and bind using your favorite method.

## Inspiration

Minnesota is a beautiful state, but it's really the people and their "Minnesota Nice" attitude that won me over. The folks we met while traveling through the state were friendly, generous and welcoming. Everywhere we went, it just felt like we were getting a big warm hug. The spirit of this place left more of an impression than any particular landscape or visual aspect could, so the Minnesota Throw was inspired by the people of this beautiful state.

THE NEW MEXICO QUEEN QUILT was fully inspired by the beautiful culture of New Mexico. The colors are borrowed from the turquoise jewelry that's pervasive in the region, bright red chiles and earthy adobe. The design is a modern reimagination of traditional Navajo rug designs. The design may look complex, but when you break it down into halves, then rows, then blocks, you can make more sense of it. The HSTs in this quilt create a lot of direction and movement. To create a focal point to harness that movement, but still allow the energy of the design to flow, I decided on a radiating V shape for the quilting. This is one of my favorite quilting designs, and it works perfectly with the New Mexico Queen Quilt.

# NEW MEXICO QUEEN QUILT

90 x 90" (228.6 x 228.6 cm)

| Fabric | Yardage | # of Pieces | Dimensions |
|---|---|---|---|
| Black | 7 yards (6.4 m) | 12 | 9 x 9" (22.9 x 22.9 cm) |
| | | 9 | 2½" (6.3 cm) x WOF |
| | | 2 | 94" (238.8 cm) x WOF |
| Terracotta | ½ yard (0.5 m) | 8 | 9 x 9" (22.9 x 22.9 cm) |
| Gold | ¾ yard (0.7 m) | 12 | 9 x 9" (22.9 x 22.9 cm) |
| Seafoam | ¾ yard (0.7 m) | 12 | 9 x 9" (22.9 x 22.9 cm) |
| Natural | 4⅔ yards (4.3 m) | 44 | 9 x 9" (22.9 x 22.9 cm) |
| | | 12 | 8½ x 8½" (21.6 x 21.6 cm) |
| | | 2 | 82½ x 5½" (209.5 x 14 cm) |
| | | 2 | 90½ x 5½" (229.9 x 14 cm) |
| Batting | | 96 x 96" (243.8 x 243.8 cm) | |

**Step 1.1**

Cutting diagram — **44" (1.1 m)** tall:

| | |
|---|---|
| 90.5 x 5.5" (229.9 x 14 cm) | 9" (22.9 cm) ×6 · 8.5" (21.6 cm) ×3 |
| 90.5 x 5.5" (229.9 x 14 cm) | 9" (22.9 cm) ×6 · 8.5" (21.6 cm) ×3 |
| 82.5 x 5.5" (209.5 x 14 cm) | 9" (22.9 cm) ×6 · 8.5" (21.6 cm) ×3 |
| 82.5 x 5.5" (209.5 x 14 cm) | 9" (22.9 cm) ×6 · 8.5" (21.6 cm) ×2 |
| 9" (22.9 cm) ×10 | 9" (22.9 cm) ×6 · 8.5" (21.6 cm) ×2 |
| 9" (22.9 cm) ×10 | 9" (22.9 cm) ×6 · 8.5" (21.6 cm) ×2 |

# Step 1: Cut the Fabric

1. Cut your fabric based on the chart on page 81. To make the most of your Natural fabric, cut according to the diagram above.

2. Set your 2½" (6.3-cm) Black strips and 94" (238.8-cm) x WOF Black fabric aside with the rest of your leftover fabric.

# Step 2: Make the Half Square Triangles (HSTs)

1. This pattern is made up of 88 half square triangles, so you'll start by making all your HSTs. For detailed photos and tips on making two-at-a-time HSTs, refer to the Technique Tutorial on page 57. All 88 HSTs have a Natural background, so take each of your 9" (22.9-cm) Black, Terracotta, Gold and Seafoam squares, mark a crease diagonally from corner to corner, place each square on top of a 9" (22.9-cm) Natural square and pin on either side of the crease. Repeat until all the colored squares are matched and pinned to a Natural square. You should have 44 total.

2. Then, you'll sew ¼" (6 mm) to the left of the crease, using the edge of your presser foot as a guide. Because you're sewing so many HSTs at once, I'd recommend chain piecing. That means that once you've sewn the first square, pause for a moment without breaking your thread to grab the next square and feed it through your machine with that same ¼" (6 mm) left of the crease. Continue until you've sewn to the left side of the crease on all 44 squares. At the end, snip your threads, flip your chain of squares around and repeat on the other side of the crease.

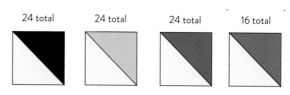

24 total   24 total   24 total   16 total

**Step 2.2**

3. When all your squares have been sewn on both sides of the crease, snip the threads connecting each square. Then, using your ruler and rotary cutter, cut along each crease. You'll want to press your seams open before trimming each square down to 8½ x 8½" (21.6 x 21.6 cm). You should end up with 24 Black + Natural HSTs, Seafoam + Natural HSTs and Gold + Natural HSTs, and 16 Terracotta + Natural HSTs.

# Step 3: Assemble the Quilt Top

1. When all the HSTs are assembled, you'll be ready to put them all together to create the overall design. I found it easiest to piece two HSTs together at a time, especially because there are only eight variations. Then you'll sew these pairs together to create each row before sewing the rows together to create the finished top.

2. Starting with Pair A, take two Black HSTs, orient them as pictured to the right, then flip the right HST over on top of the left HST with their right sides facing each other. Sew along the right edge, and repeat using the chain piecing method until you have ten of pair A. Repeat these steps for pairs B through H, and press the seams open.

3. Next, you'll assemble the rows. This design mirrors itself on the top and bottom, so you'll be making two of each row. Use the diagram as a guide for how to put together your pairs to make all ten rows. Press your seams open.

4. When you've completed all your rows, sew the rows together along the long edge from top to bottom based on the diagram. With long rows like this where you have to match a lot of seams, it's helpful to pin the rows together at each seam to make sure the fabric doesn't shift while sewing. Because the design mirrors itself, you'll create two identical halves and then sew those together.

5. When you've finished sewing all your rows together, sew the 82½" (209.5-cm) long Natural strips onto the right and left side, then sew the 90½" (229.9-cm) long Natural strips onto the top and bottom.

## Step 4: Finish the Quilt

1. Sew your scraps together into a strip that's 94" (238.8 cm) long and at least 8" (20.3 cm) wide. Then sew the two pieces of backing fabric to either side of your scrap strip along the long edge. Press the seams open.

2. Following the steps outlined in Building a Quilt on page 15, press all your seams open, and iron to smooth the quilt top and backing fabric. Baste, quilt and bind using your favorite method.

### ▶ Inspiration

I've been visiting New Mexico since I was young, and I fall in love with the Land of Enchantment more every time. The culture is so rich, its people are proud in the most humble way and the landscape is beautiful. But it's the design, the architecture and the food that stand out most to me and are what inspired the New Mexico Queen Quilt.

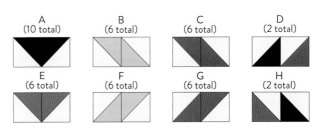

Step 3.2

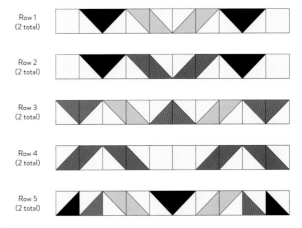

Step 3.3

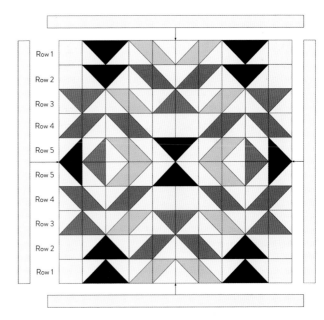

Step 3.5

# DESIGN NOTES

## Thinking About Color

Simple geometric quilts stand apart from many traditional quilts by using a limited solid color palette. Solid colors accentuate the shapes, making them the main focus of the design. There are no printed fabrics or complex quilting patterns to distract from the geometric shapes that make up the quilt. I usually work with three to five colors in a quilt and, when in doubt, always go with a neutral background.

Choosing colors can be an overwhelming part of the design process. My first couple trips to the craft store to choose fabrics took forever; I was completely paralyzed by choice. Without a clear vision of what I wanted, I spent hours standing in front of the hundreds of fabrics. It's taken some time to refine the colors I like to work with, but now I have narrowed down a palette of colors that I know I love, I know they work well together, and I can use the same colors in different combinations over and over again. I revisit these colors once a year to add in new hues I'm drawn to or take some out if I haven't used them. This creates a cohesive look to my work and keeps choosing colors stress-free.

I take my inspiration for color from many places—nature, architecture, art, brands I admire, beautiful interiors, natural dyes, photography and travel. I'm always gathering images I find beautiful or color combinations that are particularly inspiring on Pinterest and Instagram. After a while, you start to see patterns emerge, the same colors or tones repeating and your style forming. Make note of these colors, find them in fabric form and use often!

Because I use Robert Kaufman's Kona Cottons regularly, I bought one of their color cards, which has small swatches of all 340 of their Kona fabric colors. I cut it up into individual tiles so I can put different colors together and make different palettes. To keep them organized, I arranged the tiles by color family and store them in a small box, but keep my preferred palette separate so I can easily find the colors I use often. You can create your own swatch library using scraps of fabric.

# Taking It to the Next Level with Curves

# INCORPORATING CURVES IN MY WORK

has been as challenging as it has been satisfying. There's something about the shape of a half circle or an inset circle in a quilt that's unexpected, gentle and pleasing—elements that you can't get from other shapes. I consider it an intermediate-level sewing skill, but I encourage you to try it out and take some time to practice. There's a bit of a learning curve when it comes to piecing curves, but once you get the hang of the technique, you'll be hooked!

The variety of shapes and effects you can get from a simple curve expands what you can create in a distinctly modern quilt. Curves can express shapes found in nature that straight lines can't. Capturing the sunrise and sunset in the Rise + Set Throw (page 107), the gentle curve of the weathered rock formations in the Arches Queen Quilt (page 113), or the rounded tumbling stones in the Sand Dollar Table Runner (page 99) wouldn't be possible without a curve.

In this section, you'll learn how to make quarter circles, half circles, double half circles and inset circles. If you're just getting started with curves, I recommend reading through the Technique Tutorial (page 89) and practicing the techniques on some scrap fabric to get the feel for it. When you feel confident, the quarter circles in the Altamont Pillow (page 95) and the large-scale half circles in the Yuba Crib Quilt (page 103) will ease you into the rest of the projects in this chapter.

# TECHNIQUE TUTORIAL

## Quarter Circles, Half Circles and Inset Circles

In this chapter, all five projects will be based on quarter circles, half circles and inset circles. To create these shapes, you'll need templates in a variety of sizes. You can buy premade acrylic templates, but making your own is so simple and doesn't require any special tools. Once you learn this method, you'll be able to make curves in any size you'd like!

## Making Templates

### Tools

- Sheet of thick paper or cardboard that's at least the same length as your curve's diameter (I like to use either butcher paper or a cardboard shipping box)
- Ruler
- Pen or pencil
- Scissors

## 1. Mark the Diameter

1. Place your paper or cardboard flat on your workspace and using your ruler along the straight edge of the paper, mark the length of the diameter. If you're making a 12½" (31.7-cm) template, make a mark at 0" (0 cm) and 12 ½" (31.7 cm).

## 2. Mark the Radius

1. Then you want to find the radius, or the halfway point, by dividing the diameter by two. 12½" (31.7 cm) divided by two is 6¼" (15.9 cm), so you'll make a mark along the straight edge of the paper at 6¼" (15.9 cm) halfway between the 0" (0 cm) and 12½" (31.7 cm). Then, from that mark, draw a 6¼" (15.9 cm), long radius line straight up from that mark, perpendicular to the straight edge.

## 3. Draw the Curve

1. Keeping your ruler centered at the halfway point, move the end of the ruler around the half circle like a clock and draw multiple radius lines that radiate out from the center. Once you can see the half circle shape forming, use your pencil to connect the ends of each radius line, making a smooth curved line from the 0" (0-cm) mark up to the 6¼" (15.9 cm) and down to the 12½" (31.7-cm) mark. It doesn't have to be perfect, but making sure it's a fairly smooth and even curve will make for easier piecing.

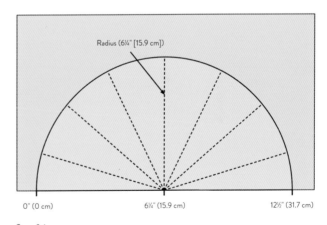

*Step 3.1*

## 4. Cut Out the Template

1. Once you're happy with your drawn half circle, cut out the template with your scissors. Make sure to label your template with the diameter so you don't get them mixed up!

Template sizes for the projects in this book:

- Template A: 18½" (47 cm)

- Template B: 17½" (44.5 cm)

- Template C: 9½" (24.1 cm)

- Template D: 8½" (21.6 cm)

- Template E: 12½" (31.7 cm)

- Template F: 11½" (29.2 cm)

- Template G: 24½" (62.2 cm)

- Template H: 23½" (59.7 cm)

- Template I: 8½" (21.6 cm)

- Template J: 7½" (19 cm)

> Note: When you piece curves, you have two pieces of fabric that require two different sized templates: one will become the actual half circle (or quarter circle or inset circle) and the other will be the background (with a half circle cut out of it). In order to account for the ¼" (6-mm) seam allowance, the diameter of the half circle template must measure 1" (2.5 cm) larger than the background template's diameter. If you need the finished size of your half circle to be a specific dimension, say 12" (30.5 cm), you'll need a 12½" (31.7-cm) half circle template and an 11½" (29.2-cm) background template.

*Half circles and inset circles take your sewing skills and quilt designs to the next level.*

## Quarter Circles and Half Circles

Both quarter circles and half circles use the same technique, but quarter circles tend to be a little easier if you're just starting out. Because they're pieced the same way, I'll show you how to construct a half circle since it's used more frequently in the book. Keep in mind that everything is the same for quarter circles, but you're just using one half of the template to cut out your quarter circles.

Let's use a 12" (30.5-cm) half circle for an example. You'll need the following fabric and templates.

- Template E (12½" [31.7 cm])

- Template F (11½" [29.2 cm])

- Dark Blue Rectangle (6½ x 12½" [16.5 x 31.7 cm])

- Terracotta Rectangle (6½ x 12½" [16.5 x 31.7 cm])

I'll show you how to make a Terracotta circle on a dark blue background. The larger of the two templates will always be used for the half circle itself. The smaller template will be used to cut the concave half circle out of the rectangle you're inserting the half circle into.

You have one Terracotta rectangle you'll use for the half circle and one Dark Blue rectangle for the background that are both 6½ x 12½" (16.5 x 31.7 cm). Place Template E on top of your Terracotta rectangle, lining up the straight edge of the template with the bottom edge of the fabric, and carefully cut around the template. Keep the half circle, and discard the surrounding rectangle. Do the same with Template F and your Dark Blue rectangle, being more careful to center the template. Discard the half circle, and keep the surrounding rectangle.

Cut around the template.

 Note: Sewing with curves can be tricky and there's a steep learning curve before getting the hang of the technique. I'd recommend practicing with scrap fabric and giving yourself some grace.

To piece your half circle into the background, place both pieces in front of you on your workspace. Orient both so the flat edge (the side you cut from) is facing away from you. Then align the right edge of the Terracotta half circle with the left edge of the Dark Blue concave curve.

Start slowly sewing along the edge of the curve with a ¼" (6-mm) seam allowance, adjusting every ½" (12 mm) to keep both pieces together so the curved edges meet as you move around the curve. Note that the Terracotta half circle won't be flat—as long as the fabric underneath your presser foot is flat and pucker-free, you're doing it right! Don't be afraid to stop and readjust multiple times. When you reach the end of the half circle, you may need to stop and lift the presser foot to bring the two ends together.

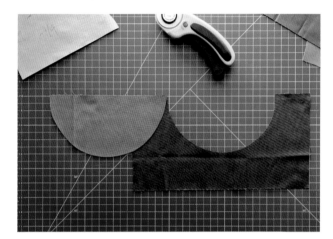

Place each piece for piecing.

Move the edges of the curves together while sewing.

When you've sewn all the way around the half circle, press your seam outwards toward the dark blue background. If the bottom edges don't line up perfectly, just trim the bottom.

 Tip: You'll want to keep both the top and bottom fabrics at a slight tension while you're sewing around the curve to keep both flat. Don't pull too much or you'll warp the half circle. Depending on the fabric you choose, it may be worth it to test out one or two half circles before starting your project.

## Inset Circles

An inset circle is a circular piece of fabric sewn into a hole in another piece of fabric. It's a bit trickier and less forgiving than half circles since there's a better chance of puckering, but the effect is impressive. I'll show you how to make a 12" (30.5-cm) Curry inset circle on a Charcoal background.

You'll need the following fabric and templates:

- Template E (12½" [31.7 cm])

- Template F (11½" [29.2 cm])

- Curry square (12½ x 12½" [31.7 x 31.7 cm])

- Charcoal square (18½ x 18½" [47 x 47 cm])

*Patience makes perfect when it comes to sewing a half circle.*

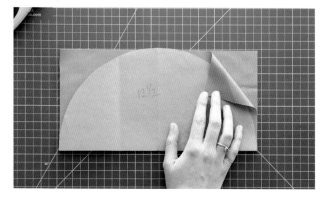

*Cut out the circle.*

Place your Curry square on your cutting mat and fold it in half. Place Template E on top of the folded square, lining up the straight edge of the template with the folded edge of the fabric, and carefully cut around the template. Unfold your Curry square and you should have a perfect circle. Using the same method, cut a circle out of the center of your Charcoal square with Template F. Because this square is larger than your template, make sure the template is centered. Discard the circle you cut out, and keep the surrounding square with a hole in the center.

Next, you'll sew the Curry circle into your Charcoal square. Fold both pieces of fabric into quarters and make a crease at each fold. Lay out your Curry circle on your workspace, then place your Charcoal square on top of the circle, centering the hole over the circle and lining up the creases. Find your first crease on the Charcoal square and flip that edge over so that the right sides are facing, lining up both curved edges and aligning the creases. Pin in place. Do the same with the remaining 3 creases.

This will keep your circle from getting too wonky and help to keep your fabric evenly spaced. Then, with the Curry circle on the bottom, slowly sew along the edge with a ¼" (6-mm) seam allowance, adjusting the fabric to bring the curved edges together as you go. You'll sew all the way around your circle, adjusting how taut you're pulling each piece of fabric in order to avoid any puckering.

When you're finished, press your seams outwards, toward the Charcoal square.

*Pin the fabric together, right sides facing at each crease.*

*Carefully sew around the circle, adjusting the curved edges together while sewing.*

QUARTER CIRCLES ARE the perfect introduction to curves. They're more forgiving than half circles or inset circles, so if you're just starting out with curves, I recommend the Altamont Pillow for your first project. Using golden-hued quarter circles in different orientations mimics the rolling hills surrounding the Altamont Pass outside San Francisco, creating a sense of movement and forward motion. This design is really versatile—play around with the orientation of the quarter circles and try out some different fabrics to create a whole new design.

# ALTAMONT PILLOW

14 x 24" (35.6 x 61 cm)

| Fabric | Yardage | # of Pieces | Dimensions |
|---|---|---|---|
| Flax Linen (Yarn Dyed) | 1 yard (1 m) | 6 | 6½ x 6½" (16.5 x 16.5 cm) |
| | | 2 | 4½ x 12½" (11.4 x 31.7 cm) |
| | | 2 | 2½ x 26½" (6.3 x 67.3 cm) |
| | | 2 | 14½ x 16" (36.8 x 40.6 cm) |
| Wheat | ¼ yard (0.2 m) | 2 | 6½ x 6½" (16.5 x 16.5 cm) |
| Curry | ¼ yard (0.2 m) | 2 | 6½ x 6½" (16.5 x 16.5 cm) |
| Yarrow | ¼ yard (0.2 m) | 1 | 6½ x 6½" (16.5 x 16.5 cm) |
| Gold | ¼ yard (0.2 m) | 1 | 6½ x 6½" (16.5 x 16.5 cm) |
| Batting | 16 x 26" (40.6 x 66 cm) | | |
| Pillow Insert | 16 x 26" (40.6 x 66 cm) | | |

## Step 1: Cut the Fabric

1. Using your rotary cutter, ruler and cutting mat, cut all your fabric according to the table. Set the two 14½ x 16" (36.8 x 40.6-cm) Flax rectangles aside for assembling the pillow back later.

## Step 2: Cut the Curves

1. Make the following templates using the method on page 90:

• Template E (12½" [31.7 cm])

• Template F (11½" [29.2 cm])

2. You'll use one half of these templates to trace the curves onto your fabric. Refer to the Technique Tutorial on page 89 for detailed steps, photos and helpful tips on how to piece curves.

3. Place one of your Flax squares on your cutting mat and position the left half of Template F on top, lining up the straight edge of the template with the bottom edge of your square. You'll want to leave ½" (12 mm) of the fabric hanging out of the left side (see diagram). Carefully cut around the template, keep the surrounding rectangle, and discard the quarter circle. Repeat with the rest of your Flax squares.

4. Take your Wheat, Curry, Yarrow and Gold squares. Using the left half of Template E, line up the straight edge of the template with the bottom edge of your square. Carefully cut around the template. Don't worry about leaving the ½" (12 mm) of fabric hanging out. Discard the surrounding squares, and keep the quarter circles.

## Step 3: Piece the Curves

1. Place one Flax square in front of you so that the two straight uncut sides are on the bottom and left. Place a Wheat quarter circle on top with the two straight sides oriented on the top and left, and align the top right edge of the Wheat quarter circle with the top of the inset curve in the Flax square.

2. Slowly sew along the edge with a ¼" (6-mm) seam allowance, adjusting both pieces as you go to align the edges as you sew around the curve. Repeat with the rest of your Flax squares and quarter circles until you have six total. Press your seams inwards toward the center of the quarter circles. Then trim your quarter circle blocks down to 6½ x 6½" (16.5 x 16.5 cm), making sure to leave a ¼" (6-mm) allowance on the Flax squares.

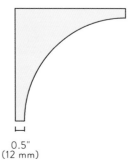

0.5"
(12 mm)

*Step 2.3*

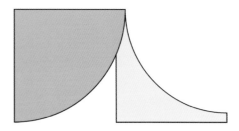

*Step 3.1*

## Step 4: Assemble the Pillow Top

1.  Using the diagram, sew two rows of three quarter circle blocks together, making sure to orient them correctly. Press the seams open. Then, before sewing the two rows together along the long edge, align the seams and pin to keep in place while sewing.

2.  To complete your pillow top, sew the two 4½ x 12½" (11.4 x 31.7-cm) Flax rectangles to the short sides of your quarter circle block. Press the seams open, and then sew the two 2½" (6.3-cm) Flax strips to the top and bottom to finish.

## Step 5: Finish the Pillow

1.  Press all your seams open, and iron to smooth the pillow top and backing fabric. The backing fabric will be on the inside of the pillow, so feel free to use any 16 x 26" (40.6 x 66-cm) piece of fabric you have. Following the steps on page 19, baste and quilt using your favorite method, then trim your top down to 14½ x 24½" (36.8 x 62.2 cm).

2.  Take the two 14½ x 16" (36.8 x 40.6-cm) Flax rectangles and hem each piece along the short edge. To do that, fold the edge over ½" (12 mm) and press flat. Then fold another ½" (12 mm) and press. Sew along the edge of your first fold, securing the hem.

3.  Next, place your pillow on your workspace with the right side facing up. Take one of your hemmed backing pieces and place it on top with the right side (the smooth side of the hem) facing down. Line up the raw short edge with the right side of your pillow top. Do the same with your other backing piece, but align the raw short edge with the left side of the pillow top. Your two backing pieces should overlap by a few inches. Pin around the edges, and sew with a ¼" (6-mm) seam allowance all the way around the rectangle. Then trim the corners at an angle to reduce bulk, and turn your pillow right side out. Stuff with a 16 x 26" (40.6 x 66-cm) pillow insert and you're done!

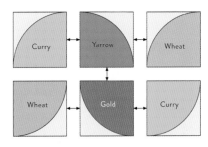

*Step 4.1*

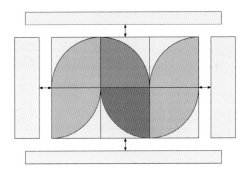

*Step 4.2*

## Inspiration

The Altamont Pass is a few miles of road that runs through bare golden hills covered in windmills. It connects the cool San Francisco Bay Area to the warm Central Valley. We'd drive over this pass to go camping in the Sierras or leave for a road trip, so the Altamont Pass became synonymous with going on an adventure.

**THE SAND DOLLAR TABLE RUNNER** uses textured fabrics as different types of rocks, and it uses a repeating shape oriented differently to mimic the rocks rolling in and out of the surf. This runner is all about the movement of the rocks in the surf of the beach, and I wanted to capture that movement with vertical and horizontal quilting for the coordinating orientations of the half circles. Keeping the quilting and fabric minimal and classic for this table runner was important; it doesn't overpower the dinner table, when the stars should be the food, the conversation and the company.

# SAND DOLLAR TABLE RUNNER

12 x 64" (30.5 x 162.6 cm)

| Fabric | Yardage | # of Pieces | Dimensions |
|---|---|---|---|
| Charcoal | 1 yard (0.9 m) | 2 | 2½ x 64½" (6.3 x 163.8 cm) |
| | | 2 | 2½ x 8½" (6.3 x 21.6 cm) |
| | | 10 | 5 x 9" (12.7 x 22.9 cm) |
| | | 5 | 4½ x 8½" (11.4 x 21.6 cm) |
| | | 4 | 2½" (6.3 cm) x WOF |
| Natural Linen (Homespun) | ⅛ yard (0.1 m) | 3 | 4½ x 8½" (11.4 x 21.6 cm) |
| Charcoal Linen (Homespun) | ⅛ yard (0.1 m) | 3 | 4½ x 8½" (11.4 x 21.6 cm) |
| Flax Linen (Yarn Dyed) | ⅛ yard (0.1 m) | 2 | 4½ x 8½" (11.4 x 21.6 cm) |
| Steel Linen (Yarn Dyed) | ⅛ yard (0.1 m) | 2 | 4½ x 8½" (11.4 x 21.6 cm) |
| Batting | 14 x 66" (35.6 x 167.6 cm) | | |

## Step 1: Cut the Fabric

1. Using your rotary cutter, ruler and cutting mat, cut all your fabric according to the chart on page 99. Set the 2½" (6.3-cm) charcoal strips and leftover fabric aside for later.

## Step 2: Cut the Curves

1. Make the following templates using the method on page 89:

   - Template I (8½" [21.6 cm])
   - Template J (7½" [19 cm])

2. You'll use these templates to trace the curves onto your fabric. Refer to the Technique Tutorial on page 89 for detailed steps, photos and helpful tips on how to piece curves.

3. Start by cutting the half circles out of all your Flax, Steel, Natural and Charcoal Linen rectangles. Place your first rectangle on your cutting mat and position Template I on top, lining up the straight edge with the long edge of the rectangle. Carefully cut around the template, keep the half circle and discard the surrounding rectangle. Repeat with the rest of your rectangles until you have ten half circles.

4. Then, following the same steps as above, take your 5 x 9" (12.7 x 22.9-cm) Charcoal rectangles with Template J, center the template on the long edge of the rectangle and carefully cut around the template. Keep the surrounding rectangle, and discard the half circle. Repeat with all ten Charcoal rectangles.

## Step 3: Piece the Curves

1. Take one half circle and one Charcoal rectangle, orient both pieces so the flat edge is facing away from you and align the right edge of the half circle with the left edge of the Charcoal inner curve. Slowly sew along the edge with a ¼" (6-mm) seam allowance, adjusting both pieces as you go to align the edges as you sew around the curve. Repeat with the rest of your half circles and Charcoal rectangles until you have ten total. Press your seams outwards and away from the center of the half circles. Then trim your half circle blocks down to 4½ x 8½" (11.4 x 21.6 cm).

## Step 4: Assemble the Runner

1. Take the three Natural and two Steel half circle blocks and sew a 4½ x 8½" (11.4 x 21.6-cm) Charcoal rectangle onto each base of the half circles. Press those seams open.

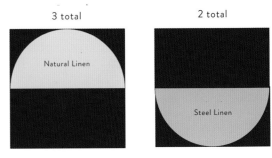

3 total        2 total

Natural Linen

Steel Linen

*Step 4.1*

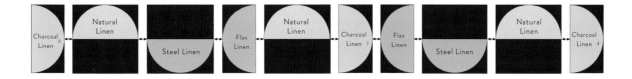

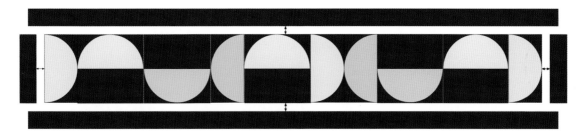

*Step 4.2*

2. Following the diagram above, sew the half circle blocks and half circle + rectangles together, paying attention to the orientation. To finish the runner, sew both 2½ x 8½" (6.3 x 21.6-cm) Charcoal strips onto the two short edges of your runner, then sew the two long Charcoal strips onto the long sides.

## Step 5: Finish the Table Runner

1. Use the leftover remnants from your quilt top to create the back of your runner, sewing them into a long piece that's at least 14 x 66" (35.6 x 167.6 cm).

2. Following the steps on page 15, press all your seams open, and iron to smooth the quilt top and backing fabric. Baste, quilt and bind using your favorite method.

## Inspiration

Sand Dollar Beach is a large, crescent-shaped beach in Big Sur that I try and visit every time I'm driving up Highway 1 along the California coast. It's usually foggy and cool, and the beach is made up of smooth tumbled rocks instead of sand. Last time I was there, we sat and listened to the waves pushing and pulling these rocks back and forth in the surf, making a soothing clacking sound of rocks rolling over each other. It's one of those sounds that I recall when I'm stressed or overwhelmed—it instantly calms me and puts me at ease.

THIS MINIMALIST DESIGN makes the Yuba Crib Quilt a quick project, and the large-scale half circles are perfect for getting comfortable with curves. Because the Yuba Crib Quilt is so minimal and focuses on the three half circles, I wanted to mix up the quilting design and give the sense of diving into the Yuba swimming holes with Vs that point downwards. The bold blue backing fabric reminds me of the clear skies overhead on a hot summer day.

# YUBA CRIB QUILT

30 x 39" (76.2 x 99.1 cm)

| Fabric | Yardage | # of Pieces | Dimensions |
|---|---|---|---|
| Flax Linen (Yarn Dyed) | 1¼ yards (1.2 m) | 2 | 24½ x 12½" (62.2 x 31.7 cm) |
| | | 1 | 24½ x 9½" (62.2 x 24.1 cm) |
| | | 2 | 33½ x 3½" (85.1 x 8.9 cm) |
| | | 2 | 30½ x 3½" (77.5 x 8.9 cm) |
| Seafoam | ½ yard (0.5 m) | 1 | 12½ x 6½" (31.7 x 16.5 cm) |
| | | 4 | 2½" (6.3 cm) x WOF |
| Army Green | ⅓ yard (0.3 m) | 1 | 18½ x 9½" (47 x 24.1 cm) |
| Evergreen | ½ yard (0.5 m) | 1 | 24½ x 12½" (62.2 x 31.7 cm) |
| Medium Blue | 1 yard (0.9 m) | | |
| Batting | 34 x 43" (86.4 x 109.2 cm) | | |

## Step 1: Cut the Fabric

1. Using your rotary cutter and ruler, cut your fabric based on the chart on page 103. Set aside your backing and binding fabric for later.

## Step 2: Cut the Curves

1. Make the following templates using the method on page 89. You'll use these templates to trace the curves onto your fabric.

   • Template A (18½" [47 cm])

   • Template B (17½" [44.5 cm])

   • Template E (12½" [31.7 cm])

   • Template F (11½" [29.2 cm])

   • Template G (24½" [62.2 cm])

   • Template H (23½" [59.7 cm])

2. Place a 24½ x 12½" (62.2 x 31.7-cm) Flax rectangle on your cutting mat and position Template B on top, centering the template and lining up the straight edge with the long edge of the rectangle. Carefully cut around the template, keep the surrounding rectangle and discard the half circle. Repeat with the other 24½ x 12½" (62.2 x 31.7-cm) Flax rectangle using Template H. Do the same with your smaller 24½ x 9½" (62.2 x 24.1-cm) Flax rectangle and Template F.

3. Then, following the same steps above, take your Evergreen rectangle and Template G and carefully cut around the template. Keep the half circle, and discard the surrounding rectangle. Do the same with the Army Green and Template B, then the Seafoam and Template E.

## Step 3: Piece the Curves

1. Start by piecing your large Evergreen half circle into the inner curve of the Flax rectangle with the largest half circle cut out. Refer to the Technique Tutorial on page 89 for detailed steps, photos and helpful tips on how to piece curves. Orient both pieces so the flat edge is facing away, and align the right edge of the Evergreen half circle with the left edge of the Flax inner curve. Slowly sew along the edge with a ¼" (6-mm) seam allowance, adjusting both pieces as you go to align the edges as you sew around the curve. Repeat with the Army Green and Seafoam half circles and the corresponding Flax rectangles. Press your seams outwards and away from the center of the half circles.

## Step 4: Complete the Quilt Top

1. Sew the three curve blocks together along the long edge according to the assembly diagram. Press the seams upwards toward the top of the quilt. Then sew the two 33½" (85.1-cm) strips to the left and right side of that block and finally, sew the 30½" (77.5-cm) strips to the top and bottom to complete your quilt top.

## Step 5: Finish the Quilt

1. Following the steps on page 15, press all your seams, and iron to smooth the quilt top and backing fabric. Baste, quilt and bind using your favorite method.

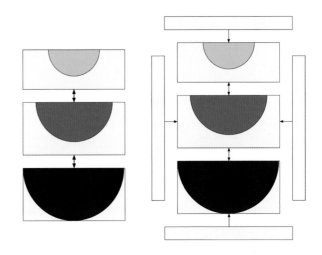

Step 4.1

## Inspiration

The Yuba River that runs through the foothills of the Sierras is the epitome of summer swimming holes. Huge limestone boulders dot the tree-lined river and create pools of different depths that range from deep blue green to light turquoise. On any given day in the summertime, you can find families, friends and couples going for a dip and sunning themselves on the giant limestone boulders. It's a special place to me (it's where my husband proposed!), and I always love going back.

**THE RISE + SET THROW** captures the duality, movement and colors of the rising and setting sun. The half circles and double half circles use the same technique, but are slightly more advanced. I love the pattern it creates, and the versatility of the design. To balance out the many curves in the Rise + Set Throw, I chose vertical rows of stitches for the quilting pattern. This connects the rows, grounds the pattern and adds a different textural element.

# RISE + SET THROW

60 x 60" (152.4 x 152.4 cm)

| Fabric | Yardage | # of Pieces | Dimensions |
|---|---|---|---|
| Natural | 3½ yards (3.2 m) | 18 | 20½ x 10½" (52.1 x 26.7 cm) |
| | | 2 | 54½ x 3½" (138.4 x 8.9 cm) |
| | | 2 | 60½ x 3½" (153.7 x 8.9 cm) |
| Dark Blue | 1½ yards (1.4 m) | 9 | 18½ x 9½" (47 x 24.1 cm) |
| Cayenne | 1 yard (0.9 m) | 9 | 9½ x 5" (24.1 x 12.7 cm) |
| | | 6 | 2½" (6.3 cm) x WOF |
| Wheat | ½ yard (0.5 m) | 9 | 9½ x 5" (24.1 x 12.7 cm) |
| Indigo Linen (Homespun) | 3 yards (2.75 m) | 1 | 64" (162.6 cm) x WOF |
| | | 2 | 22" (55.9 cm) x WOF |
| Batting | 64 x 64" (162.6 x 162.6 cm) | | |

## Step 1: Cut the Fabric

1.  Using your rotary cutter, ruler and cutting mat, cut all of your fabric into designated pieces according the chart on page 107. Set aside the 2½" (6.3-cm) Cayenne strips for your binding. Trim the selvedge off your Indigo fabric, and set aside to use for the quilt back.

## Step 2: Cut the Curves

1.  Make the following templates using the method on page 89. You'll use these templates to trace the curves onto your fabric.

    *   Template A (18½" [47 cm])

    *   Template B (17½" [44.5 cm])

    *   Template C (9½" [24.2 cm])

    *   Template D (8½" [21.6 cm])

2.  Place a 20½ x 10½" (52.1 x 26.7-cm) Natural rectangle on your cutting mat and position Template B on top, centering the template and lining up the straight edge with the long edge of the rectangle. Carefully cut around the template, keep the surrounding rectangle and discard the half circle. Repeat with half of your 20½ x 10½" (52.1 x 26.7-cm) Natural rectangles until you have nine total.

3.  With your remaining nine Natural rectangles, use Template D to cut out smaller half circles using the same steps above. Discard the half circles, and keep the surrounding rectangles.

4.  Take your Dark Blue rectangles and Template A to cut out nine half circles, and discard the surrounding rectangles. Then take Template D and center it on the bottom edge of your half circle. Cut around the template. Discard the small half circle, and you should end up with a U shape.

Step 2.2–2.5

Step 2.6

5.  For the Cayenne and Wheat rectangles, use Template C to cut half circles. Discard the surrounding rectangle. You should end up with nine of each shape.

6.  Start by piecing your Wheat half circles into the small inner curve of the Dark Blue U. Refer to the Technique Tutorial on page 89 for detailed steps, photos and helpful tips on how to piece curves. Orient the Dark Blue U so the flat edge is facing away from you. Take your Wheat half circle with the flat edge facing away and align the right edge with the left edge of the small inner curve. Slowly sew along the edge with a ¼" (6-mm) seam allowance, adjusting both pieces as you go to align the edges as you sew around the curve. Repeat with all your Wheat and Dark Blue pieces until you have nine total.

7. Repeat step 6 to insert the Dark Blue + Wheat half circles into the Natural rectangle with the larger half circle cut out. Make sure the right sides are facing as you're piecing. You should end up with nine blocks. Press your seams outwards and away from the center of the half circle, and then trim your blocks down to 18½ x 9½" (47 x 24.1 cm).

8. Follow step 6 to piece your Cayenne half circles into the Natural rectangle with the smaller half circle cut out. Repeat until you have nine blocks total. Press your seams outwards and away from the center of the half circle, and then trim your blocks down to 18½ x 9½" (47 x 24.1 cm).

## Step 3: Complete the Quilt Top

1. To create the blocks that will make up this quilt top, place one of your Dark Blue + Wheat blocks with the base of the half circle facing up and place a Cayenne + Natural block on top with the right sides facing. Line up the seams of the Wheat and Cayenne half circles, and pin in place. Sew along the long edges of the rectangle to join the half circles. Unfold, and press your seams open. Repeat to join the rest of your blocks until you have nine total.

2. When your blocks are complete, sew three blocks together in a row, rotating the middle one the opposite way. Make sure to line up the center seams and pin together to keep the blocks in place while you sew.

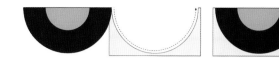

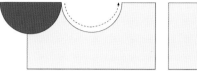

*Step 2.7*

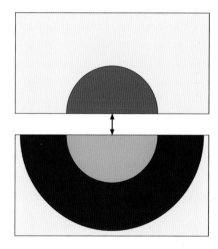

*Step 2.8*

*Step 3.1*

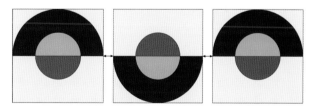

*Step 3.2*

3. After you've created three rows of three identical blocks, press your seams open, then sew each row together as pictured in the assembly diagram, making sure to line up your seams. When all three rows are sewn together, sew both 54½" (138.4-cm) Natural strips to the right and left side, then sew both 60½" (153.7-cm) Natural strips to the top and bottom. Press your seams open, and your quilt top is complete!

## Step 4: Finish the Throw

1. Sew the short edges of the two small pieces of backing fabric together. Then sew that piece to the larger piece of backing fabric to along the long edge. Press the seams open.

2. Following the steps outlined on page 15, press all your seams open, and iron to smooth the quilt top and backing fabric. Baste, quilt and bind using your preferred method.

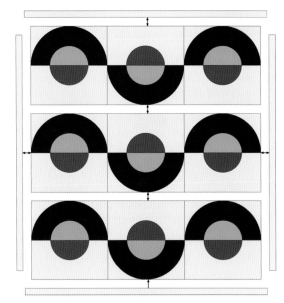

Step 3.3

## Inspiration

Watching the sun rise and set is a universal joy. There's something about starting and finishing the day with natural beauty that has no substitute. During an impromptu camping trip to Big Sur, we pitched our tent on a roadside pullout in the hills overlooking Highway 1 and the Pacific Ocean. Watching the sun sink into the ocean and then waking up as it was rising over the wild hills was one of the more memorable experiences of the sun's rise and set.

**THE ARCHES QUEEN QUILT** is inspired by the colors and shapes of the rock formations that make Arches National Park in Moab, Utah, so incredible. The combination of large-scale inset circles and double half circles makes this queen-size quilt as impressive as it is simple. While the techniques are more advanced, the construction is minimal and fun to put together. For large quilts with lots of negative space like this, mixing fabrics and including a textured yarn-dyed linen adds visual interest and a depth that would otherwise be lacking with cotton alone. Plus it's super cozy and looks amazing on a bed! The straight quilting rows are the easiest and quickest way to quilt a large piece like this, but it's also modern, minimal and timeless.

# ARCHES QUEEN QUILT
90 x 90" (228.6 x 228.6 cm)

| Fabric | Yardage | # of Pieces | Dimensions |
|---|---|---|---|
| Indigo Linen (Yarn Dyed) | 6½ yards (6 m) | 2 | 90½ x 9½" (229.9 x 24.1 cm) |
| | | 2 | 54½ x 9½" (138.4 x 24.1 cm) |
| | | 4 | 27½ x 27½" (69.9 x 69.9 cm) |
| | | 10 | 18½ x 9½" (47 x 24.1 cm) |
| | | 6 | 9½ x 9½" (24.1 x 24.1 cm) |
| Terracotta | 1¾ yards (1.6 m) | 4 | 18½ x 18½" (47 x 47 cm) |
| | | 9 | 2½" (6.3 cm) x WOF |
| Paprika | 2 yards (1.9 m) | 12 | 9½ x 5" (24.1 x 12.7 cm) |
| | | 6 | 18½ x 9½" (47 x 24.1 cm) |
| Gold | 5¼ yards (4.8 m) | 2 | 94" (238.8 cm) x WOF |
| Batting | 96 x 96" (243.8 x 243.8 cm) | | |

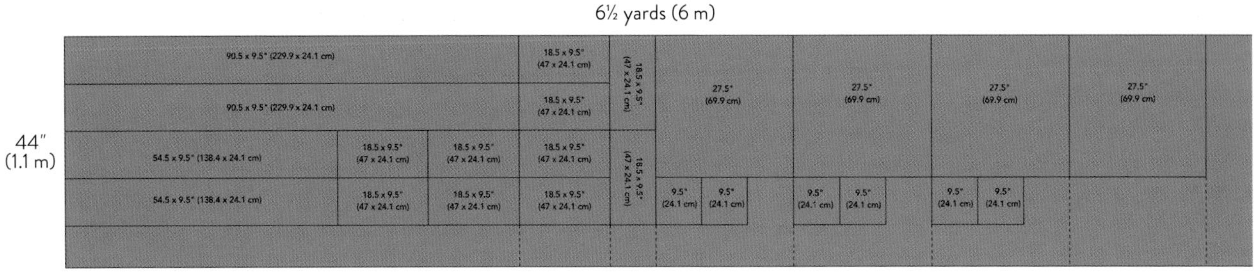

Step 1.1

The cutting diagram at top shows fabric measurements:

6½ yards (6 m)

90.5 x 9.5" (229.9 x 24.1 cm)
90.5 x 9.5" (229.9 x 24.1 cm)
54.5 x 9.5" (138.4 x 24.1 cm)
54.5 x 9.5" (138.4 x 24.1 cm)

18.5 x 9.5" (47 x 24.1 cm) — multiple pieces

44" (1.1 m)

27.5" (69.9 cm) — multiple squares

9.5" (24.1 cm) — multiple small squares

## Step 1: Cut the Fabric

1. Start by cutting your Indigo fabric using the chart on page 113 and the diagram above in order to take full advantage of your yardage.

2. Cut your Terracotta and Paprika fabrics into designated pieces according the chart on page 113. Cut the Gold quilt back fabric in half and trim selvedge off. Set aside with your 2½" (6.3-cm) Terracotta strips for the binding and your leftover fabric for later.

## Step 2: Cut the Curves

1. Make the following templates using the method on page 89. You'll use these templates to trace the curves onto your fabric.

   - Template A (18½" [47 cm])
   - Template B (17½" [44.5 cm])
   - Template C (9½" [24.2 cm])
   - Template D (8½" [21.6 cm])

2. Place one of your 18½" (47-cm) Terracotta squares on your cutting mat and fold it in half. Place your Template A on top of the folded square, lining up the straight edge of the template with the folded edge of the fabric, and carefully cut around the template. Unfold your Terracotta square, and you should have a perfect circle. Repeat with the remaining three Terracotta squares.

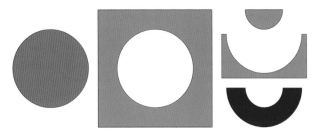

Step 2.2–2.5

3. Using the same method as the previous steps, cut circles out of the center of your four 27½" (69.9-cm) Indigo squares with Template B. Because the square is larger than your template, make sure the template is centered. Discard the circle you cut out, and keep the surrounding square with a hole in the center.

4. Take your 18½ x 9½" (47 x 24.1-cm) Paprika rectangle. Using Template A, line up the bottom edges and cut around the template. Discard the surrounding rectangle, and keep the half circle you cut out. Then take Template D, center it on the bottom edge of your half circle and cut around the template. Discard the small half circle, and you should end up with a U shape. Repeat with the remaining five Paprika rectangles.

5. Repeat the steps above with six of your 18½ x 9½" (47 x 24.1-cm) Indigo rectangles using Template B, keeping the surrounding rectangle. Take Template C and line it up with the bottom edge of the half circle you cut out, then cut around the template. Discard the larger half circle, and keep the small half circle.

## Step 3: Piece the Curves

1. Start by piecing your small Indigo half circles into your small Paprika inner curve. Refer to the Technique Tutorial on page 89 for detailed steps, photos and helpful tips on how to piece curves. Orient your Paprika half circle so the flat edge is facing away from you. Take your small Indigo half circle with the flat edge facing away and align the right edge with the left edge of the small Paprika inner curve. Slowly sew along the edge with a ¼" (6-mm) seam allowance, adjusting both pieces as you go to align the edges as you sew around the curve. Repeat with the remaining small Indigo half circles.

2. Repeat the steps above to insert the Paprika half circles into the 18½ x 9½" (47 x 24.1-cm) Indigo inner curves. You should end up with six blocks. Press your seams outwards and away from the center of the half circle, and then trim your blocks down to 18½ x 9½" (47 x 24.1 cm).

3. Next, you'll sew the Terracotta circles into your large Indigo square using the Inset Circles method detailed on page 92. Fold both pieces of fabric into quarters and make a crease at each fold. Lay out your Terracotta circle on your workspace, then place your Indigo square on top of the circle, centering the hole over the circle and lining up the creases. Find your first crease on the Indigo square and flip that edge over, lining up both curved edges and aligning the creases. Pin in place. Do the same with the remaining three creases. This will keep your circle from getting too wonky and help to keep your fabric evenly spaced. Then, with the Terracotta circle on the bottom, slowly sew along the edge with a ¼" (6-mm) seam allowance, adjusting the fabric to bring the edges together as you go. Repeat with the remaining three Terracotta circles and Indigo squares, and press the seams outwards.

## Step 4: Complete the Quilt Top

1. To create the bottom legs of the Paprika Us, take one of the 9½" (24.1-cm) Indigo squares and sew two 9½ x 5" (24.1 x 12.7-cm) Paprika rectangles to opposite sides of the square. Repeat this for the remaining Indigo squares, and press your seams outwards toward the Paprika rectangles.

2. Now you can attach the bottom legs to the Paprika half circles you pieced earlier. With right sides facing and making sure to align the seams where the Paprika and Indigo fabrics meet, sew along the long edge to create a block that looks like the diagram. Repeat with all your bottom legs and Paprika half circles. Press your seam open.

3. To create the two rows of Paprika Us, sew three Paprika Us together with a 18½ x 9½" (47 x 24.1-cm) Indigo rectangle between each U. Repeat to make another identical row.

Step 3.1

Step 3.2

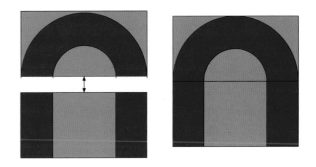

Step 4.2

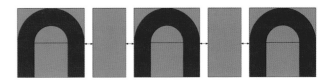

Step 4.3

4. Take your inset Terracotta circles and sew the four squares together to create a larger square.

5. To finish, sew the two 54½" (138.4-cm) Indigo strips to the top and bottom of the Terracotta circles block. Then sew the two Paprika U rows to the right and left sides of the block you just created. Finally, sew the 90½" (229.9-cm) strips on to the top and bottom to complete your quilt top.

## Step 5: Finish the Quilt

1. Sew your scraps together into a strip that's 94" (238.8 cm) long and at least 8" (20.3 cm) wide. Then sew the two pieces of Gold backing fabric to either side of your scrap strip along the long edge. Press the seams open.

2. Following the steps outlined on page 15, press all your seams open, and iron to smooth the quilt top and backing fabric. Baste, quilt and bind using your favorite method.

### Inspiration

Visiting Arches National Park in Moab, Utah, kind of blew me away: the bright red-orange color of the rows, the precarious-looking arches that seemed structurally unsound and the sheer scale of these rock formations, worn away slowly by the elements. Double Arch was the most impressive iteration of all, with its two delicate rock arches looming high above the desert floor. The Arches Queen Quilt mimics these rock formations in shape and color, with a textured linen background the color of the sky.

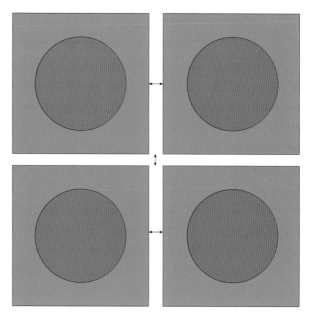

Step 4.4

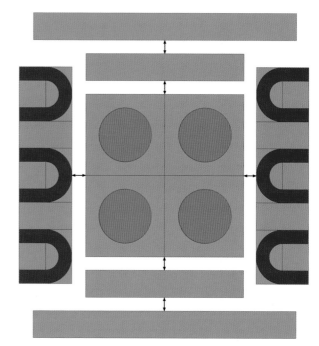

Step 4.5

# DESIGN NOTES

## Quick Intro to Quilt Math

If you want to try your hand at designing your own quilts or even just making a quilt pattern in a different size, you'll need to know the basics of quilt math.

I know, just the word "math" can be intimidating. But I promise this is the easy kind. If you start simple and learn the basics, you'll be able to design and scale any quilt pattern!

You'll need graph paper, a pencil and a calculator to get started. Let's begin with a simple pattern, the Montara Wall Hanging (page 67).

Draw out the design on your graph paper, making sure each triangle is two squares wide and two squares tall. Then count how many squares tall and wide the finished wall hanging is: it should be 12 squares wide by 16 squares long. Because this is a small wall hanging, I've decided the scale should be 1 square = 1 inch (2.5 cm). That means the finished wall hanging will be 12 x 16" (30.5 x 40.6 cm). If I wanted to make it into a crib quilt, I can make the scale 1 square = 3 inches (7.6 cm). I multiply the width by 3 (12" [30.5 cm] x 3 = 36" [91.4 cm]) and the length by 3 (16" [40.6 cm] x 3 = 54" [137.2 cm]), so my crib quilt will be 36 x 54" (91.4 x 137.2 cm). You can use this method to make any size quilt you'd like!

When you have your scale determined, you'll need to figure out the pieces of the quilt. I like to make my life easy and keep things simple, so I've decided that the Montara is 24 half square triangles total, sewn together in four columns of six HSTs with a border around the edges. Sometimes it's helpful to draw dotted lines to distinguish the separate pieces in the design.

Now that we've figured out the shapes of the pieces, we need to find the dimensions. Each triangle is two squares, and the finished dimensions of each HST will be 2 x 2" (5 x 5 cm). Add on ¼" (6 mm) for the seam allowance on all sides and your starting dimension of each HST will be 2½ x 2½" (6.3 x 6.3 cm). Because I make two-at-a-time HSTs (see page 57) where the rule is finished dimension + 1" (2.5 cm), you'll want your fabric squares to be 3 x 3" (7.6 x 7.6 cm).

Time to determine how many of each piece! Let's keep things simple and make all the HSTs the same color. So that means there are 24 blue triangles and 24 white triangles. Because I make those two-at-a-time HSTs, you'll divide 24 by 2 and get 12. So I want to cut twelve 3 x 3" (7.6 x 7.6-cm) blue pieces and twelve 3 x 3" (7.6 x 7.6-cm) white pieces.

For the border, it's just four rectangles. Each rectangle measures 2 squares by 12 squares, so your finished rectangles are 2 x 12" (5 x 30.5 cm) and with your ¼" (6-mm) seam allowances, the starting dimensions you'll cut is 2½ x 12½" (6.3 x 31.7 cm).

When you're scaling your design up, just remember to multiply your finished dimensions by your scale and add the ½" (12 mm) to account for your seam allowances. For example, with the crib quilt that has a scale of 1 square = 3" (7.6 cm), those 2½ x 12½" (6.3 x 31.7-cm) rectangles would be 6½ x 36½" (16.5 x 92.7 cm).

That's it! You've learned the basics of quilt math! Keep in mind, the more complicated your design, the more complicated the math can be. Keeping things simple when you're first starting out is the way to go.

Combining Shapes for Dynamic Quilts

COMBINING SQUARES, triangles and curves into one quilt design makes for a distinctly contemporary quilt. It's a unique style that isn't restrained by the traditional method of repeating blocks. There's a freedom in combining geometric shapes suspended in the quilt's negative space that leans more toward the design world. And because the shapes are larger and construction is made as uncomplicated as possible, these projects come together quickly and make a bold statement.

Because you have all the geometric shapes at your disposal, you can get really creative. Take for example, the Purifoy Wall Hanging (page 127). It's a jumble of squares, rectangles, curves and colors combined into a piece that's playful and a little wild, but totally cohesive. Or the Virgin River Throw (page 137), where the tonal rectangles are enveloped by white half circles. The designs are more dynamic, like the Oregon Crib Quilt (page 133), which represents the three distinct climates of the state, or the Tent Rocks Pillow (page 123) that's impactful despite only using two shapes.

The projects in this chapter take all the techniques you learned for squares, rectangles, triangles and curves and combines them into cohesive quilts, pillows and wall hangings. If you're unfamiliar with any of the techniques in these projects, refer back to the previous chapters.

**THE TENT ROCKS PILLOW** incorporates half rectangle triangles and curves to create an unexpected, minimalist design inspired by Kasha-Katuwe Tent Rocks National Monument in New Mexico. This simple design is impactful and unique, and it can be modified to accommodate your favorite color palette. Using smaller projects, such as pillows or wall hangings, to try out more complex quilting methods is a great way to experiment with style and technique.

# TENT ROCKS PILLOW

18 x 18" (45.7 x 45.7 cm)

| Fabric | Yardage | # of Pieces | Dimensions |
|---|---|---|---|
| Natural Linen (Homespun) | ½ yard (0.5 m) | 1 | 10 x 19" (25.4 x 48.3 cm) |
| | | 3 | 4 x 10½" (10.2 x 26.7 cm) |
| Wheat | ¾ yard (0.7 m) | 1 | 6½ x 12½" (16.5 x 31.7 cm) |
| | | 2 | 18½ x 14" (47 x 35.6 cm) |
| Peach | ⅛ yard (0.1 m) | 3 | 4 x 10½" (10.2 x 26.7 cm) |
| Batting | 20 x 20" (50.8 x 50.8 cm) | | |
| Pillow Insert | 20 x 20" (50.8 x 50.8 cm) | | |

## Step 1: Cut the Fabric

1.  Using your rotary cutter, ruler and cutting mat, cut all your fabric according to the chart on page 123. Set the two 18½ x 14" (47 x 35.6-cm) Wheat rectangles aside for assembling the pillow back later.

## Step 2: Cut the Curves

1.  Make the following templates using the method on page 89. You'll use these templates to trace the curves onto your fabric.

    *   Template E (12½" [31.7 cm])

    *   Template F (11½" [29.2 cm])

2.  Place the Natural rectangle on your cutting mat and center Template F on the long edge of the rectangle, lining up the straight edge of the template with the bottom edge of your square. Carefully cut around the template, keep the surrounding rectangle and discard the half circle.

3.  Then, using Template E, line up the straight edge of the template with the bottom edge of your Wheat rectangle and carefully cut around the template. Discard the surrounding square, and keep the half circle.

## Step 3: Piece the Curves

1.  Start by piecing your half circle and refer to the Curves Technique Tutorial on page 89 for detailed steps, photos and helpful tips on how to piece curves.

2.  Take your Wheat half circle and Natural rectangle, orient both pieces so the flat edge is facing away from you and align the right edge of the half circle with the left edge of the inner curve. Slowly sew along the edge with a ¼" (6-mm) seam allowance, adjusting both pieces as you go to align the edges as you sew around the curve. Press your seams outwards and away from the center of the half circles. Then, to make sure all your corners and edges are straight and squared away, trim the block down to 10 x 19" (25.4 x 48.3 cm).

## Step 4: Assemble the Half Rectangle Triangles

1.  Refer to the Half Rectangle Technique Tutorial on page 58 for detailed steps, photos and helpful tips on how to make HRTs.

2.  Start by cutting your Natural and Peach rectangles diagonally from top right to bottom left corner. Then organize your triangles into stacks of three, oriented like the diagram.

3.  Take one Natural triangle (90-degree corner at the top left) and one Peach triangle (90-degree corner at the bottom right), flip the Peach triangle on top of the Natural so right sides are facing and the long edges align. The points should overlap by ¼" (6 mm). Sew along the longest edge with a ¼" (6-mm) seam allowance, then press the seam open. Repeat to make two more identical HRTs. Then, with the triangles oriented the opposite way, follow the previous steps to make three more HRTs.

*Step 3.2*

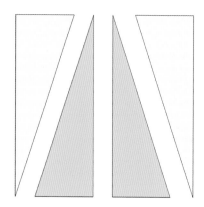

*Step 4.2*

3 total          3 total

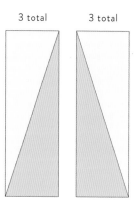

*Step 4.3*

4. When you've made all six HRTs, trim each one down to 3⅔ x 10" (9.3 x 25.4 cm).

## Step 5: Complete the Pillow Top

1. Start by sewing your HRTs together in pairs until you have three Tent Rocks. You'll want to take one of each HRT and sew down the long Peach edge to create one Tent Rock. Then sew those three Tent Rocks together along the long edges so all the points are facing the same direction. Press all your seams open.

2. Then sew the half circle block to the long edge of the HRT block. Press your seams open, and your pillow top is finished!

## Step 6: Finish the Pillow

1. Press all your seams open, and iron to smooth the pillow top and backing fabric. The backing fabric will be on the inside of the pillow, so feel free to use any 20 x 20" (50.8 x 50.8-cm) piece of fabric you have. Following the steps on page 16, baste and quilt using your favorite method, then trim your top down to 18½ x 18½" (47 x 47 cm).

2. Take the two pieces of Wheat pillow back fabric and hem each piece along the longest edge. To do that, fold the edge over ½" (12 mm) and press flat. Then fold another ½" (12 mm) and press. Sew along the edge of your first fold, securing the hem.

3. Next, place your pillow on your workspace with the right side facing up. Take one of your hemmed backing pieces and place it on top with the right side (the smooth side of the hem) facing down. Line up the raw long edge with the top and sides of your pillow top. Do the same with your other backing piece, but align the long raw edge with the bottom of the pillow top. Your two backing pieces should overlap by a few inches. Pin around the edges, and sew with a ¼" (6-mm) seam allowance all the way around the square. Then trim the corners at an angle to reduce bulk, and turn your pillow right side out. Stuff with a 20 x 20" (50.8 x 50.8-cm) pillow insert and you're done!

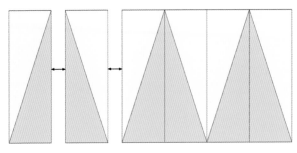

*Step 5.1*

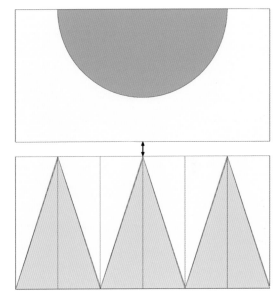

*Step 5.2*

## Inspiration

Kasha-Katuwe Tent Rocks National Monument sits between Albuquerque and Santa Fe on Native American land. There's a short but challenging hike that takes you through slot canyons and twists around these pillars of rocks worn down to look like tents. The trail ends on a plateau high above the ground, giving you a view of the Tent Rocks from above. The design for the Tent Rocks Pillow is a simple distillation of those rocks, with the warm New Mexico sun above.

THE PURIFOY WALL HANGING was directly inspired by a Noah Purifoy sculpture at his outdoor museum in Joshua Tree, California. I love how playful and adaptable this wall hanging is. It's the perfect project for using leftover fabric scraps, and you can create endless color palettes. Because there's so much going on already, I kept the background quilting simple with vertical rows, but kept it fun with a splash of hand quilting for extra texture.

# PURIFOY WALL HANGING

16 x 17" (40.6 x 43.2 cm)

| Fabric | Yardage | # of Pieces | Dimensions | Name |
|---|---|---|---|---|
| Charcoal (Homespun) | ½ yard (0.5 m) | 1 | 7 x 18" (17.8 x 45.7 cm) | C1 |
| | | 1 | 7 x 12" (17.8 x 30.5 cm) | C2 |
| | | 1 | 1½ x 1½" (3.8 x 3.8 cm) | C3 |
| | | 2 | 1½ x 3½" (3.8 x 8.9 cm) | C4 |
| | | 2 | 1½ x 4½" (3.8 x 11.4 cm) | C5 |
| | | 1 | 1½ x 6½" (3.8 x 16.5 cm) | C6 |
| | | 1 | 2½ x 2½" (6.3 x 6.3 cm) | C7 |
| | | 1 | 2½ x 5½" (6.3 x 14 cm) | C8 |
| | | 1 | 3½ x 3½" (8.9 x 8.9 cm) | C9 |
| | | 2 | 2½" (6.3 cm) x WOF | Binding |
| Peach | ⅛ yard (0.1 m) | 1 | 4½ x 8½" (11.4 x 21.6 cm) | |
| | | 1 | 1½ x 10½" (3.8 x 26.7 cm) | |
| Army Green | ⅛ yard (0.1 m) | 1 | 4½ x 8½" (11.4 x 21.6 cm) | |
| | | 1 | 1½ x 7½" (3.8 x 19 cm) | |
| Seafoam | ⅛ yard (0.1 m) | 1 | 2½ x 4½" (6.3 x 11.4 cm) | |
| | | 1 | 2½ x 6½" (6.3 x 16.5 cm) | |
| Terracotta | ⅛ yard (0.1 m) | 1 | 4½ x 7½" (11.4 x 19 cm) | |
| | | 1 | 1½ x 3½" (3.8 x 8.9 cm) | |
| Sienna | ½ yard (0.5 m) | 1 | 5½ x 6½" (14 x 16.5 cm) | |
| | | 1 | 18 x 19" (45.7 x 48.3 cm) | Backing |
| Batting | | | 18 x 19" (45.7 x 48.3 cm) | |

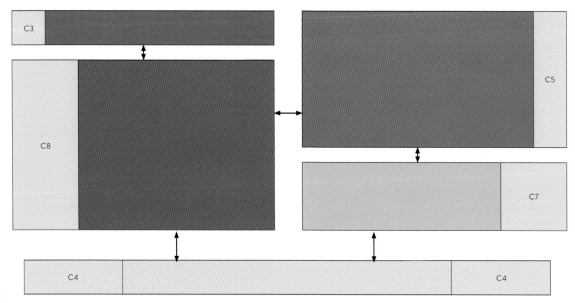

*Step 3.1*

## Step 1: Cut the Fabric

1. Using your rotary cutter, ruler and cutting mat, cut your fabric based on the chart on page 127. Set aside your backing, binding and any leftover fabric for later.

## Step 2: Cut + Piece the Curves

1. Make the following templates using the method on page 89. You'll use these templates to trace the curves onto your fabric.

   • Template I (8½" [21.6 cm])

   • Template J (7½" [19 cm])

2. Stack both of your large Peach and Army Green rectangles and position Template I on top, lining up the straight edge with the long edge of the rectangle. Carefully cut around the template, keep the half circles and discard the surrounding rectangles.

3. Take the largest C1 rectangle and center Template J on the long edge of the rectangle, and carefully cut around the template. Keep the surrounding rectangle, and discard the half circle. Do the same with C2, but position the template ½" (12 mm) from the short left edge so the half circle is to the left of center.

4. To piece the two half circles, start with C1 and the Army Green half circle and orient both pieces so the flat edges are facing away from you. Refer to the Curves Technique Tutorial on page 89 for detailed steps, photos and helpful tips on how to piece curves. Align the right edge of the Army Green half circle with the left edge of the C1 inner curve. Slowly sew along the edge with a ¼" (6-mm) seam allowance, adjusting both pieces as you go to align the edges as you sew around the curve. Repeat with the C2 rectangle and Peach half circle. Press your seams outwards and away from the center of the half circles. Then trim the rectangles down to 5½ x 16½" (14 x 41.9 cm) for C1 and 5½ x 10½" (14 x 26.7 cm) for C2.

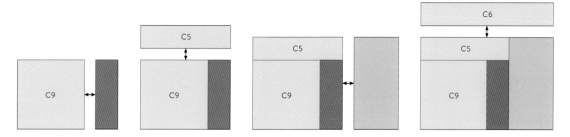

*Step 3.2*

## Step 3: Assemble the Blocks

1.  Using the diagrams above and to the left, sew the five colored rectangles to their corresponding Charcoal rectangles, making sure they're sewn onto the correct side. Press the seams open. Then sew the Army Green + Charcoal pair to the top edge of the Sienna pair. Sew the Terracotta pair to the top edge of the Seafoam pair. Press your seams open, then sew those two blocks together as pictured in the diagram. The last step is to sew the Peach trio onto the bottom edge of the block. Press all your seams open.

2.  Next, starting with your small Terracotta rectangle and C9, use the diagram to sew the C5, small Seafoam and C6 rectangles together, pressing the seams open as you go.

## Step 4: Complete the Quilt Top

1.  Using the diagram, sew the block you just created to the left edge of the Peach half circle block. Press the seams open, then sew that block to the top side of the previous block you assembled. To complete the wall hanging top, sew the Army Green half circle block onto the bottom side of the previous block. Press all your seams open.

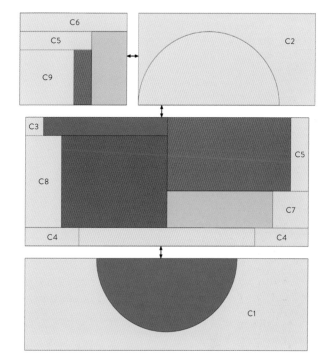

*Step 4.1*

## Step 5: Finish the Wall Hanging

1. Following the steps on page 15, press all your seams open, and iron to smooth the quilt top and backing fabric. Baste and quilt using your favorite method.

2. Before binding your wall hanging, cut two 4 x 4" (10.2 x 10.2-cm) squares out of any leftover fabric: these will become the tabs at the top corners to mount your wall hanging. Fold each square in half diagonally, and press at the fold to create two triangles. On the back side of your wall hanging, place each triangle in the top two corners, lining up the corners and the short legs with the edge of the wall hanging. Pin in place. Then sew a scant ¼" (6-mm) seam allowance along the top and side of both triangles. These stitches will be covered by your binding.

3. Bind following the method on page 24.

4. To mount your wall hanging, insert a wooden dowel that's 1" (2.5 cm) shorter than the width of your wall hanging. Use one or two nails or a removable adhesive strip to mount on the wall.

Step 5.2

## Inspiration

There's an open air museum in the high desert town of Joshua Tree, California, that showcases the life's work of artist and sculptor Noah Purifoy. It's ten acres of assembled found objects turned art—some of it funny, some disturbing, some incredibly moving and inspiring. All with the backdrop of the desert. The one large piece that really stood out to me was a stack of geometric shapes made out of corrugated metal, propped up on legs. The Purifoy Wall Hanging was inspired by those seemingly random shapes that fit together so perfectly, and it uses the colors of a desert sunset.

**THE OREGON CRIB QUILT** combines all three geometric techniques into a unisex quilt that would look at home in a crib or hanging on the wall. It represents a variety of landscapes found within this magical state—coast, forest and desert—represented by three different geometric shapes—curves, triangles and rectangles. Each shape is quilted in a unique way to highlight the unique sections. This crib quilt is a quick project that's perfect for practicing the different techniques featured in each chapter.

# OREGON CRIB QUILT

32 x 46" (81.3 x 116.8 cm)

| Fabric | Yardage | # of Pieces | Dimensions |
|---|---|---|---|
| Natural | 1¼ yards (1.2 m) | 1 | 32½ x 20½" (82.6 x 52 cm) |
| | | 1 | 32½ x 2½" (82.6 x 6.3 cm) |
| | | 2 | 32½ x 4½" (82.6 x 11.4 cm) |
| | | 3 | 7 x 7" (17.8 x 17.8 cm) |
| | | 2 | 10½ x 6½" (26.7 x 16.5 cm) |
| | | 1 | 8½ x 6½" (21.6 x 16.5 cm) |
| Yarrow | ½ yard (0.5 m) | 1 | 12½ x 12½" (31.7 x 31.7 cm) |
| Spice | ¼ yard (0.2 m) | 2 | 32½ x 2½" (82.6 x 6.3 cm) |
| Army Green | ¼ yard (0.2 m) | 3 | 7 x 7" (17.8 x 17.8 cm) |
| Indigo Linen (Homespun) | 1⅔ yards (1.5 m) | 1 | 36 x 50" (91.4 x 127 cm) |
| | | 4 | 2½" (6.3 cm) x WOF |
| Batting | 36 x 50" (91.4 x 127 cm) | | |

## Step 1: Cut the Fabric

1. Using your rotary cutter, ruler and cutting mat, cut all your fabric according to the chart on page 133. Set the Indigo fabric for your binding and backing fabric aside for later.

## Step 2: Cut + Piece the Inset Circle

1. Make the following templates using the method on page 89. You'll use these templates to trace the curves onto your fabric.

   - Template E (12½" [31.7 cm])

   - Template F (11½" [29.2 cm])

2. Place the Yarrow square on your cutting mat and fold it in half. Place Template E on top of the folded square, lining up the straight edge of the template with the folded edge of the fabric, and carefully cut around the template. Unfold, and discard the surrounding rectangle. You should have a perfect circle.

3. Using the same method above, cut the circle out of the center of your 32½ x 20½" (82.6 x 52.1-cm) Natural rectangle with Template F. Because the square is larger than your template, make sure the template is centered. Discard the circle you cut out, and keep the surrounding square with a hole in the center.

4. Next, you'll sew that Yarrow circle into your Natural rectangle using the Inset Circles method detailed on page 92. Fold both pieces of fabric in quarters and make a crease at each fold. Lay out your Yarrow circle on your workspace, then place the Natural rectangle on top of the circle, centering the hole over the circle and lining up the creases. Find your first crease on the Natural rectangle, flip that edge over to the opposite side, lining up both curved edges and making sure both creases align and pin in place. Do the same with the remaining three creases. This will keep your circle from getting too wonky and help to keep your fabric evenly spaced. Then, with the Yarrow circle on the bottom, slowly sew along the edge with a ¼" (6-mm) seam allowance, adjusting the fabric to bring the edges together as you go. Press your seams outwards and away from the center of the circle.

## Step 3: Make the HST Section

1. For detailed photos and tips on making two-at-a-time HSTs, refer to the Technique Tutorial on page 57.

2. Starting with your three Army Green squares, mark a crease diagonally from corner to corner on each square. Place each square on top of the three 7" (17.8-cm) Natural squares, lining up the edges and pinning on either side of the crease. Then sew ¼" (6 mm) to the left of the crease, using the edge of your presser foot as a guide. When you reach the end of the square, flip your square around and sew along the opposite side of the crease. Repeat with your remaining squares.

3. When all your squares have been sewn on both sides of the crease, use your ruler and rotary cutter to cut along each crease. Press your seams open before trimming each square down to 6½ x 6½" (16.5 x 16.5 cm).

4. Next, you'll sew the HSTs together to make your mountains. Take two HSTs and with right sides facing and the Army Green triangles on the bottom right, line up the edges and sew ¼" (6 mm) from the right edge. Repeat with your remaining HSTs until you have three pairs sewn together. Unfold, and press the seams open.

5. To assemble the HST section, take your 8½ x 6½" (21.6 x 16.5-cm) Natural rectangle and sew a HST pair onto opposite sides of the short ends. Then take the two 10½ x 6½" (26.7 x 16.5-cm) Natural rectangles and sew onto opposite sides of your remaining HST along the short ends. Press the seams open. To complete this section, sew the two 32½ x 4½" (82.6 x 11.4-cm) Natural strips along the long edges according to the section assembly diagram. Press your seams open.

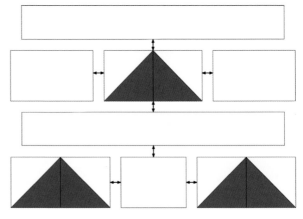

Step 3.5

## Step 4: Assemble the Stripes + Complete the Quilt Top

1. Take your two Spice strips and sew them to opposite sides of the 32½ x 2½" (82.6 x 6.3-cm) Natural strip along the long edges.

2. Then, sew the inset circle section to one side of the Spice stripes and the HST section to the other side of the Spice stripes. Press all your seams open, and your quilt top is finished!

## Step 5: Finish the Quilt

1. Following the steps outlined on page 15, press all your seams open, and iron to smooth the quilt top and backing fabric. Baste, quilt and bind using your preferred method.

### ▶ Inspiration ◀

Oregon is one of my favorite places. The combination of dramatic coastline, dry desert and mossy forested mountains in one state makes for endless exploration and always something new. This quilt represents those individual climates all in one place with a subtle nod to the classic Pendleton blanket.

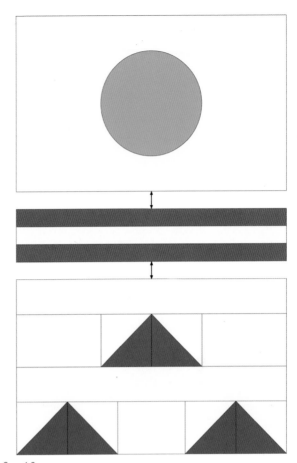

*Step 4.2*

**THE VIRGIN RIVER THROW** combines squares, rectangles and curves in the warmest tonal colors to reimagine the beauty and encompassing canyon walls of the Virgin River Gorge. Because I chose colors that are very similar to re-create the shades of the canyon walls, I wanted to use the quilting to differentiate the tones. So I focused all the quilting on the Spice and Natural fabrics, leaving the Sienna and Paprika bare. The bold and unexpected Seafoam quilt back breaks up the saturated warm colors of the front of the quilt and represents the Virgin River that runs through the canyon.

# VIRGIN RIVER THROW

54 x 72" (137.2 x 182.9 cm)

| Fabric | Yardage | # of Pieces | Dimensions |
|---|---|---|---|
| Spice | 3 yards (2.75 m) | 2 | 30½ x 12½" (77.5 x 31.7 cm) |
| | | 10 | 15½ x 12½" (39.4 x 31.7 cm) |
| | | 2 | 36½ x 6½" (92.7 x 16.5 cm) |
| | | 2 | 18½ x 6½" (47 x 16.5 cm) |
| | | 2 | 9½ x 6½" (24.1 x 16.5 cm) |
| Natural | 1 yard (0.9 m) | 2 | 18½ x 9½" (47 x 24.1 cm) |
| | | 10 | 12½ x 6½" (31.7 x 16.5 cm) |
| Paprika | 1½ yards (1.4 m) | 2 | 48½ x 6½" (123.2 x 16.5 cm) |
| | | 5 | 2½ x 54" (6.3 x 137.2 cm) |
| Sienna | ¼ yard (0.2 m) | 3 | 6½ x 6½" (16.5 x 16.5 cm) |
| Seafoam | 3¼ yards (3 m) | 2 | 58½" (148.6 cm) x WOF |
| Batting | | 58 x 76" (147.3 x 193 cm) | |

## Step 1: Cut the Fabric

1. Using your rotary cutter, ruler and cutting mat, cut all of your fabric into designated pieces according the chart on page 137. Note that with the Paprika fabric, it's best to cut along the length of the fabric instead of the usual width. Cut the Seafoam fabric in half, trim the selvedge off and set aside for later along with the 2½" (6.3-cm) Paprika strips for your binding.

## Step 2: Cut the Curves

1. Make the following templates, using the method on page 89. You'll use these templates to trace the curves onto your fabric.

   - Template A (18½" [47 cm])

   - Template B (17½" [44.5 cm])

   - Template E (12½" [31.7 cm])

   - Template F (11½" [29.2 cm])

2. Stack both 18½ x 9½" (47 x 24.1-cm) Natural rectangles on your cutting mat and position Template A on top, lining up the straight edge with the long edge of the rectangle. Carefully cut around the template, keep the half circles and discard the surrounding rectangles. You'll end up with two half circles. Repeat these steps with all ten 12½ x 6½" (31.7 x 16.5-cm) Natural rectangles and Template E.

3. Next, stack both 30½ x 12½" (77.5 x 31.7-cm) Spice rectangles on your cutting mat and position Template B on top, centering the template and lining up the straight edge with the long edge of the rectangle. Carefully cut around the template, keep the surrounding rectangles and discard the half circles. Repeat the above steps with your ten 15½ x 12½" (39.4 x 31.7-cm) Spice rectangles and Template F, making sure you're lining up your template along the 15½" (39.4-cm) side.

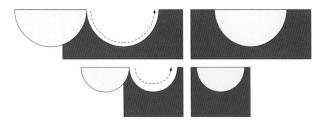

*Step 3.1*

## Step 3: Piece the Curves

1. Start by piecing your large Natural half circles into the 30½" (77.5-cm) long Spice rectangles. Refer to the Curves Technique Tutorial on page 89 for detailed steps, photos and helpful tips on how to piece curves. Orient the Spice rectangle so the cutout looks like a U. Take your Natural half circle with the flat edge facing away from you and align the Natural's right edge with the Spice's left edge of the inner curve. Slowly sew along the edge with a ¼" (6-mm) seam allowance, adjusting both pieces as you go to align the edges as you sew around the curve. Repeat with your other larger Natural half circle, and then do the same with all ten of your smaller half circles, matching them to the 15½" (39.4-cm) rectangles you cut out. Press your seams outwards and away from the center of the half circle. Trim any misshapen edges, and make sure your blocks are perfectly squared on the corners.

## Step 4: Assemble the Squares + Rectangles

1. Next, you'll sew the central squares and rectangles together to begin constructing your quilt top. Start by taking your Sienna squares and 9½ x 6½" (24.1 x 16.5-cm) Spice rectangles. Sew them together in a row, alternating Sienna and Spice. Press the seams open.

2. Next, take the two 36½" (92.7-cm) long Spice strips and sew them onto the top and bottom of your Sienna + Spice row. Press the seams open. Then you'll sew the two 18½" (47-cm) long Spice strips onto the left and right side of that block. Press all your seams open.

3. To finish this section, sew the two Paprika strips onto the top and bottom of your block. Press the seams open.

## Step 5: Complete the Quilt Top

1. Take the central squares + rectangles and your two larger half circles, and sew each half circle onto the left and right side of that block. Make sure the base of your half circles are along the edge of the quilt top.

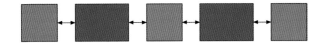

*Step 4.1*

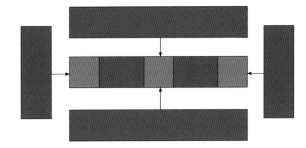

*Step 4.2*

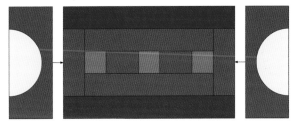

*Step 4.3*

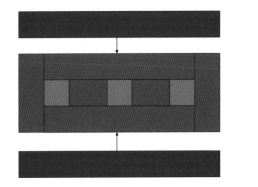

*Step 5.1*

2. To finish up your quilt top, start by sewing your smaller-pieced half circles into two rows of five half circles with all the half circles facing the same way. Press all your seams open, and then trim a 1½″ (3.8-cm) strip off each end of your row.

3. Line up the ends of the row with the ends of the block you assembled, and pin in place to ensure the fabric doesn't shift. Sew the row to the top, and then repeat on the other side of the block, making sure the base of the half circles are at the edge of the quilt top.

## Step 6: Finish the Throw

1. Sew the two pieces of Seafoam backing fabric together along the long edge. Press the seams open.

2. Following the steps outlined on page 15, press all your seams open, and iron to smooth the quilt top and backing fabric. Baste, quilt and bind using your preferred method.

*Step 5.2*

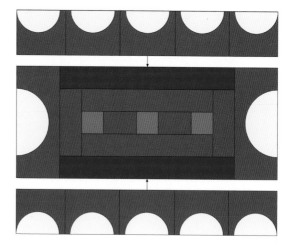

*Step 5.3*

## Inspiration

Driving through the Virgin River Gorge on the way from St. George, Utah, to Las Vegas was the most scenic road I never knew existed. It's not a destination, and there isn't much around aside from a campground and the turquoise river that runs through tall warmly colored walls of rock. But man . . . it is stunning. We camped there for one night, and to this day, it's still my favorite.

THE GOLDEN HOUR QUEEN QUILT, inspired by the magical golden hour that's amplified in coastal California, uses just two colors and two shapes to capture the simple beauty of this time of day. The central circle represents the setting sun, with half square triangles radiating outwards, casting golden light over everything. This simple design highlights the geometric shapes. The two-tone color combination and classic structure roots this quilt in tradition, but it's still quite modern, with its large-scale piecing and reliance on negative space. I wanted to give this quilt an extra special finish, so I decided on a hand-quilted diamond design that radiates out from the center, reinforcing the radiating sunbeams. And to bring a bit of shimmer and sparkle, I used a warm metallic linen for the backing and the binding.

# GOLDEN HOUR QUEEN QUILT

90 x 90" (228.6 x 228.6 cm)

| Fabric | Yardage | # of Pieces | Dimensions |
|---|---|---|---|
| Yarrow | 6 yards (5.5 m) | 2 | 90½ x 5½" (229.9 x 14 cm) |
| | | 2 | 80½ x 5½" (204.5 x 14 cm) |
| | | 2 | 64½ x 8½" (163.8 x 21.6 cm) |
| | | 2 | 48½ x 8½" (123.2 x 21.6 cm) |
| | | 24 | 8½ x 8½" (21.6 x 21.6 cm) |
| | | 16 | 9 x 9" (22.9 x 22.9 cm) |
| | | 1 | 32½ x 32½" (82.5 x 82.5 cm) |
| Natural | 1½ yards (1.4 m) | 16 | 9 x 9" (22.9 x 22.9 cm) |
| | | 1 | 18½ x 18½" (47 x 47 cm) |
| Metallic Camel Linen (Yarn Dyed) | 6⅔ yards (6.1 m) | 2 | 94" (238.8 cm) x WOF |
| | | 3 | 8½" (21.6 cm) x WOF |
| | | 9 | 2½" (6.3 cm) x WOF |
| Batting | 96 x 96" (243.8 x 243.8 cm) | | |

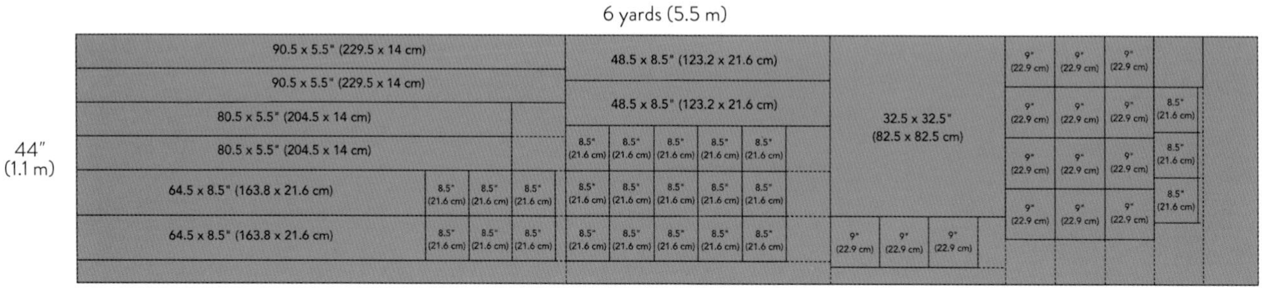

6 yards (5.5 m)

44" (1.1 m)

| 90.5 x 5.5" (229.5 x 14 cm) | | | | | 48.5 x 8.5" (123.2 x 21.6 cm) | | | | | | 9" (22.9 cm) | 9" (22.9 cm) | 9" (22.9 cm) | |
|---|---|---|---|---|---|---|---|---|---|---|---|---|---|---|
| 90.5 x 5.5" (229.5 x 14 cm) | | | | | 48.5 x 8.5" (123.2 x 21.6 cm) | | | | | | 9" (22.9 cm) | 9" (22.9 cm) | 9" (22.9 cm) | 8.5" (21.6 cm) |
| 80.5 x 5.5 (204.5 x 14 cm) | | | | | | | | | | 32.5 x 32.5" (82.5 x 82.5 cm) | 9" (22.9 cm) | 9" (22.9 cm) | 9" (22.9 cm) | 8.5" (21.6 cm) |
| 80.5 x 5.5 (204.5 x 14 cm) | | | | 8.5" (21.6 cm) | 8.5" (21.6 cm) | 8.5" (21.6 cm) | 8.5" (21.6 cm) | 8.5" (21.6 cm) | | | 9" (22.9 cm) | 9" (22.9 cm) | 9" (22.9 cm) | 8.5" (21.6 cm) |
| 64.5 x 8.5 (163.8 x 21.6 cm) | 8.5" (21.6 cm) | 8.5" (21.6 cm) | 8.5" (21.6 cm) | 8.5" (21.6 cm) | 8.5" (21.6 cm) | 8.5" (21.6 cm) | 8.5" (21.6 cm) | 8.5" (21.6 cm) | | | 9" (22.9 cm) | 9" (22.9 cm) | 9" (22.9 cm) | 8.5" (21.6 cm) |
| 64.5 x 8.5 (163.8 x 21.6 cm) | 8.5" (21.6 cm) | 8.5" (21.6 cm) | 8.5" (21.6 cm) | 8.5" (21.6 cm) | 8.5" (21.6 cm) | 8.5" (21.6 cm) | 8.5" (21.6 cm) | 8.5" (21.6 cm) | 9" (22.9 cm) | 9" (22.9 cm) | 9" (22.9 cm) | | | |

*Step 1.1*

# Step 1: Cut the Fabric

1. Take full advantage of your yardage by using the chart on page 143 and the diagram above to cut the Yarrow fabric into designated pieces.

2. Cut your Natural fabric into designated pieces according the table. Cut your Metallic Camel fabric into the backing pieces and strips for the binding, trimming the selvedge off. Set the binding, backing and any leftover fabric aside for later.

# Step 2: Make the Half Square Triangles

1. Starting with your 9" (22.9-cm) Yarrow squares, mark a crease diagonally from corner to corner and place each square on top of a 9" (22.9-cm) Natural square, pinning on either side of the crease. Repeat until you've paired all your 9" (22.9-cm) squares together—there should be sixteen total. For detailed photos and tips on making two-at-a-time HSTs, refer to the Technique Tutorial on page 57.

2. Then, you'll sew ¼" (6 mm) to the left of the crease, using the edge of your presser foot as a guide. Because you're sewing so many HSTs at once, I'd recommend chain piecing. That means that once you've sewn the first square, pause for a moment and without breaking your thread, feed your next square through you machine with that same ¼" (6 mm) left of the crease. Continue until you've sewn to the left side of the crease on all sixteen squares. At the end, snip your threads, flip your chain of squares around and repeat on the opposite side of the crease.

3. When all your squares have been sewn on both sides of the crease, snip the threads connecting each square. Then, using your ruler and rotary cutter, cut along each crease. You'll want to press your seams open before trimming each square down to 8½ x 8½" (21.6 x 21.6 cm). You should end up with 32 identical half square triangles.

# Step 3: Cut + Piece the Inset Circle

1. Make the follwoing templates using the method on page 89. You'll use these templates to trace the curves onto your fabric.

   - Template A (18½" [47 cm])

   - Template B (17½" [44.5 cm])

2. Place your 18½" (47-cm) Natural square on your cutting mat, and fold it in half. Place Template A on top of the folded square, lining up the straight edge of the template with the folded edge of the fabric, and carefully cut around the template. Unfold it, and you should have a perfect circle.

3. Using the same method above, cut circles out of the center of your 32½" (82.6-cm) Yarrow square with Template B. Because the square is larger than your template, make sure the template is centered. Discard the circle you cut out, and keep the surrounding square with a hole in the center.

4. Next, you'll sew your Natural circle into your large Yarrow square using the Inset Circles method detailed on page 92. Fold both pieces of fabric into quarters and make a crease at each fold. Lay out your Natural circle on your workspace, then place your Yarrow square on top of the circle, centering the hole over the circle and lining up the creases. Find your first crease on the Yarrow square and flip that edge over to the other side, lining up both curved edges and aligning the creases. Pin in place, and repeat with the remaining three creases. This will keep your fabric evenly spaced as you sew. Then, with the Natural circle on the bottom, slowly sew along the edge with a ¼" (6-mm) seam allowance, smoothing the wrinkles and adjusting the fabric to bring the edges together as you go.

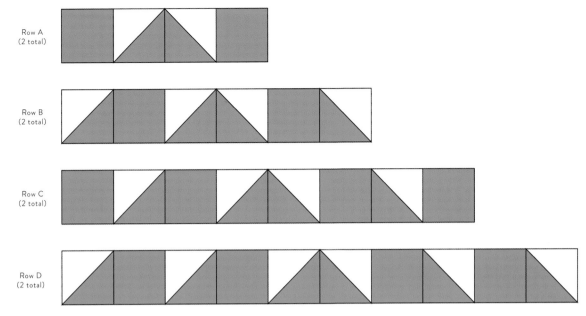

Row A
(2 total)

Row B
(2 total)

Row C
(2 total)

Row D
(2 total)

*Step 4.1*

## Step 4: Assemble the Quilt Top

1.  Start by taking your HSTs and 8½" (21.6-cm) squares and using the diagrams above as a guide, assemble two each of Rows A through D. Press your seams open.

2.  When you've sewn two of each row, you'll begin to construct the quilt top starting from the middle and working your way out. All the points of your Natural triangles should be pointing toward the center. Take your 32½" (82.5-cm) square with the inset circle and sew both Row As onto opposite sides of the square. Then, making sure your seams line up, sew each Row Bs onto the open two sides of the square. When you've sewn your Rows A and B onto the central square, use the same method to sew both 48½" (123.2-cm) Yarrow strips onto opposite sides of the square, then both 64½" (163.8-cm) Yarrow strips onto the other two sides to create a larger square.

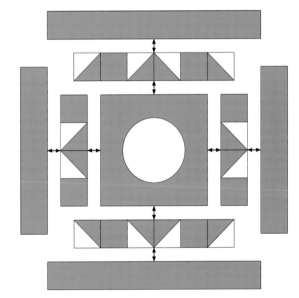

*Step 4.2*

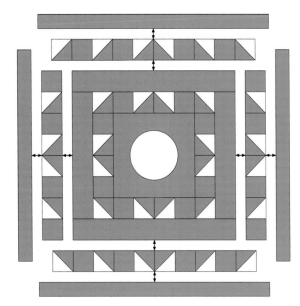

*Step 4.3*

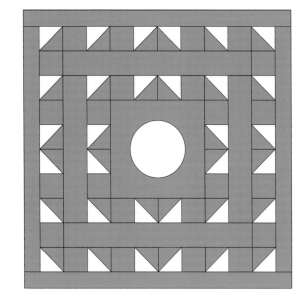

*Step 4.3*

3.  Repeat the previous steps to sew both Row Cs and Row Ds onto your growing square, then your 80½" (204.5-cm) and 90½" (229.9-cm) strips to complete your quilt top. Before sewing the longer Row C and D, it's helpful to pin the row to the square at each seam to make sure each seam at the end of the Row lines up with the seams on the square. This ensures squared corners and a neater finish.

## Step 5: Finish the Quilt

1.  Sew the two 94" (238.8-cm) x WOF Metallic Camel pieces together along the long edge, and press the seams open. Then sew all three 8½" (21.6-cm) x WOF strips together along the short edges, and press those seams open. Sew that pieced strip to the long edge of the 94" (238.8-cm) piece, press the seams open and trim the leftover fabric to square up your quilt back.

2.  Following the steps outlined on page 15, press all your seams open and iron to smooth the quilt top and backing fabric. Baste, quilt and bind using your preferred method.

## Inspiration

There's something about the California coast that amplifies the magical, golden quality of light the hour or so before sunset. It may be the sea spray floating in the air that creates atmosphere and depth of field that's unlike any other time of the day, but it's breathtakingly beautiful. Everything during that hour looks magical, almost sparkly, and it's what made me fall in love with California. The Golden Hour Queen Quilt was inspired by that glittery gold moment of the day—one that's meant to be captured and shared.

# DESIGN NOTES

## Gathering Inspiration + Making It Your Own

To gather your own inspiration, walk through the world with your eyes wide open. Take lots of photos. Write down your thoughts, things that you like and what's important to you. Collect photos of things you think are beautiful. After a while, patterns in shape and color will start to emerge and you can use that to create work that really feels like you.

If there's anything I hope you take away from this book, it's how to use what you've learned here to design and make your own quilts. I believe that everyone is creative and has the capacity to create something original: It might take some time, effort and practice, but it's absolutely possible! Don't be afraid to experiment or try something new. Even if it's just turning a quilt block a different way or creating your own color palette, it's still making the pattern your own.

# GLOSSARY

**Backstitch:** stitching one or two stitches backwards on a sewing machine in order to lock the stitch in place so that it doesn't unravel or come apart

**Basting:** when you stack the three layers of a quilt—the quilt top, batting and the backing—and pin or spray to hold the layers together

**Half Rectangle Triangle (HRT):** two triangular pieces of fabric sewn together to form a rectangle

**Half Square Triangle (HST):** two triangular pieces of fabric sewn together to form a square

**Quilt Sandwich:** the basted three layers of a quilt (the quilt top, batting and backing)

**Quilt Top:** the pieced, decorative top of a quilt

**Quilter's Knot:** a knot, typically buried under the quilt top, used to secure the end of your thread when hand quilting

**Seam Allowance:** the area between the fabric edge and the stitch line

**Selvedge:** an edge produced on woven fabric during manufacture that prevents it from unraveling

**Width of Fabric (WOF):** fabric cut from one selvage edge to the other selvage edge; cotton commonly used for quilting is 44" (111.8 cm) wide

# ACKNOWLEDGMENTS

Writing a book is not a solo endeavor—many people came together to help make *Simple Geometric Quilting* a reality, and I'm incredibly grateful for all of them.

The biggest thanks and gratitude goes to my husband, John, for his endless support and love. He's my number one cheerleader and pushes me to grow as a creative and a business owner. He also took nearly every photo in this book—I'm so grateful to have his talented eye capture my work.

The projects in this book wouldn't have happened without my team: Lindsay and Paige, who quilted and tested a handful of the quilts in this book, and my sister Emily, who helped out with a lot of boring spreadsheet work. And thank you to Christina, my dear friend and fellow lady boss, for encouraging me and talking me through this entire process.

A huge thank you to Robert Kaufman Fabrics, who generously provided all the fabric used in the book. Your fabric is always my favorite to work with!

This book would literally not have been possible without the team at Page Street Publishing and my editor, Rebecca. You took a chance on me and have pushed me to become a better writer, designer and quilter. This book has been an invaluable learning experience, as challenging as it was gratifying—thank you!

And finally, thank you to my parents, who have always supported and encouraged me, my creativity and my dreams.

# ABOUT THE AUTHOR

**Laura Preston** is an artist, designer and entrepreneur with a chronic case of wanderlust. Raised in Texas and London, Laura studied art history and painting at New York University before embarking on a year-long road trip around the United States in 2013. She's been living, working and traveling in her custom-built vintage Airstream trailer with her husband, two dogs and cat ever since.

Completely self-taught (with the help of the internet), Laura discovered the medium of textiles and quilting while traveling, and she fell in love with the utility and beauty of the craft. In February of 2015, she launched her business, Vacilando Quilting Co. Laura specializes in creating travel-inspired quilt collections, making one-of-a-kind custom pieces and collaborating with like-minded brands, artists and interior designers. She's grown Vacilando Quilting Co. organically over the years and developed a unique, recognizable style coveted by fellow quilters, travelers and clients who value quality, a minimalist aesthetic and a little adventure in life.

# INDEX